TWAYNE'S WORLD AUTHORS SERIES

A Survey of the World's Literature

Sylvia E. Bowman, Indiana University
General Editor

MEXICO

John P. Dyson, Indiana University
Editor

Carlos Fuentes

(TWAS 151)

TWAYNE'S WORLD AUTHORS SERIES (TWAS)

The purpose of TWAS is to survey the major writers—novelists, dramatists, historians, poets, philosophers, and critics—of the nations of the world. Among the national literatures covered are those of Australia, Canada, China, Eastern Europe, France, Greece, Italy, Japan, Latin America, New Zealand, Poland, Russia, Scandinavia, Spain, and the African nations, as well as Hebrew, Yiddish, and Latin Classical literature. This survey is complemented by Twayne's United States Authors Series and English Authors Series.

The intent of each volume in these series is to present a critical analytical study of the works of the writer; to include biographical and historical material that may be necessary for understanding, appreciation, and critical appraisal of the writer; and to present all material in clear, concise English —but not to vitiate the scholarly content of the work by doing so.

Carlos Fuentes

By DANIEL deGUZMAN

Queens College
of the City University of New York

Twayne Publishers, Inc.　：：　New York

Contents

Preface

Carlos Fuentes, it seems to me, is almost too much of a contemporary for his work to be critically analyzed with anything like finality. Nevertheless, he has already stirred heated controversy and partisanship among his readers, lay as well as critical, and even now it would seem indisputable that he will take his place among the important writers of Mexico. He belongs especially among those of the period of the "institutionalized Revolution"— the generation, let us say, between 1945 and the present; in other words, those born during that period of the revolutionary era that produced an amazing renaissance in almost all fields of aesthetic endeavor in Mexico.

In order to understand the forces that produced this generation, it is of course necessary to understand the historical imperatives that produced the forces themselves. Never has Ortega y Gasset's analysis of what constitutes modern mass man been more applicable. Therefore it will be my purpose in this volume on Carlos Fuentes to try to place the man and his work in their proper setting and perspective, for otherwise it will be difficult if not impossible to understand either his work or his personality.

It seems to be increasingly true that the era of collective man needs a collective background for comprehension, and by "collective background" I mean the sum of the influences—historical, social, psychological, economic, cultural—that have gone into the formation of the man and his work. It is even more important to know this total background in the case of a Mexican writer of the first half of the twentieth century, for when Carlos Fuentes was born—1928—Mexico had barely forged, in blood and civil war, a new society that was as different from the one it replaced as the France of 1800 was from that of 1780 or as the Russia of 1925 was from that of 1900.

To date, Fuentes' total production has been six novels, two books of short stories, and many articles and essays and similar journalistic work. In the approximately fifteen years of his literary productivity (his first collection of short stories was published in Mexico in 1954), he has been, while not perhaps prolific, obviously busy. I propose to consider in detail his novelistic output—after all, he is primarily a novelist—and also his short stories. His other writings, political essays, articles of literary criticism, etc., cannot be—nor need be—considered except in bulk since they are chiefly works of transitory interest, pieces written for a specific moment or with a polemical purpose. All of his work will, therefore, be considered, although not all of it will receive the thorough survey that I propose to give to his more important production.

In reviewing details of Fuentes' career, I have necessarily availed myself of an extensive bibliography not exclusively dealing with the literary aspects of his life and times. As a matter of fact, because there has been as yet comparatively little analysis in English of his work, this aspect of my presentation attempts to be an indication of the direction such criticism might logically and profitably take rather than an attempt to state definitively that this or that judgment is already appropriate. The whole thing, in conclusion, must be tentative, by the very nature of its contemporaneity.

So I try to indicate why Carlos Fuentes has done what he has done, even why he has not done that which he has left undone, and I have had to use all available sources, evaluating them as carefully as possible, in view of their own origin and purpose. My interest in the work has been that of a Mexican-American who is concerned with understanding and helping others to understand the total history of the period and particularly that aspect of it that has manifested itself in literature.

Chronology

1909   Publication of *La Sucesión Presidencial en 1910,* by Francisco I. Madero—the opening ideological gun in the movement to topple the dictator, Porfirio Díaz; the genesis of modern Mexico, of which Fuentes is a product.

1910   Beginning of the Mexican Revolution; Díaz is overthrown and goes into exile, leaving the country to Madero.

1911   Madero elected president in October; the Revolution has apparently won its objectives with little bloodshed.

1913   Madero assassinated in February as the result of a military coup engineered by Victoriano de la Huerta (supported by the American ambassador, Henry Lane Wilson). Almost immediately Venustiano Carranza, Governor of Coahuila, rises against de la Huerta and his "Federal" government; he is joined by Alvaro Obregón, Plutarco Elías Calles, Adolfo de la Huerta and, later, Pancho Villa. They organize the Constitutionalist forces and the war phase of the Revolution begins.

1914   Woodrow Wilson intervenes in April, to help Carranza; his intervention is unacceptable to all factions.

1915   Pancho Villa quarrels with Carranza and is defeated by General Alvaro Obregón outside the city of Celaya. In this same year, Mariano Azuela writes (and publishes in Texas) *Los de abjo (The Underdogs),* the first and most important "novel of the Revolution," the forerunner of the renaissance in Mexican Arts and Letters.

1917   Military victory of the Constitutional forces under Carranza and promulgation of the new Constitution; the end of the war phase of the Revolution. Carranza, as president, is urged by Luis Cabrera and Obregón to undertake a program of social reform.

1919   Emiliano Zapata ambushed and assassinated.

1920   Assassination of Carranza, after his resignation had been forced by Obregón. Obregón elected president. The beginning, in Arts and Letters, of the Mexican "renaissance," that lasts until 1940.

1923   The campaign against illiteracy, undertaken by José Vasconcelos, Minister of Education in Obregón's administration.

1924   Plutarco Elías Calles elected president.

1928   Novemebr 11: Carlos Fuentes born in Mexico City. Obregón runs again for the presidency, is reelected but is assassinated before taking office. Emilio Portes Gil is elected president but Calles rules behind the scenes until 1934.

1934   Lázaro Cárdenas elected president (for the first six-year term; the Constitution had been amended to eliminate the four-year term and make reelection impossible); he exiles Calles who goes to live in California. Fuentes goes to school as a child in Mexico City and Washington, D.C. between this year and 1950; he is also taken by his parents to Santiago (Chile), Buenos Aires, and Geneva.

1938   Expropriation of the oil industry by Cárdenas.

1952   Fuentes becomes a Marxist and joins the Communist Party; period of rebellion against his family and the middle class.

1953   Fuentes breaks with his past and gives up his career as a student of international law and diplomacy in order to be independent and a writer.

1954   Fuentes' first published book, *Los días enmascarados (The Masked Days)*, appears in Mexico: a collection of six short stories.

1956   He begins writing articles for journals.

1958   His second book and first novel, *La región más transparente,* is published in Mexico; an "experimental" work in a style new to Mexican literature.

1959   *Las buenas consciencias,* Fuentes' third book and second novel, published in Mexico; a semi-autobiographical work "in the Galdosian manner."

1960   Translation into English and publication in New York of his first novel, with the title of *Where the Air Is Clear.*

1961   Translation into English of *Las buenas consciencias* and publication in New York as *The Good Conscience.*

1962   *La muerte de Artemio Cruz,* his third novel, fourth book, in which he perfects the "experimental" technique used in

Where the Air Is Clear, published in Mexico by the prestigious Fondo de Cultura Económica: Fuentes has "arrived." His fourth novel, fifth book, *Aura*, is also published this year—a work whose theme is fantasy/reality, which will interest him more and more. He breaks with the Communist Party on intellectual grounds.

1964   Translation into English and publication of his third novel as *The Death of Artemio Cruz*. Reviewed favorably by most critics, Fuentes is established as a major international novelist. Also in this year, his sixth work, a second collection of (seven) short stories, with the title *Cantar de Ciegos* (*Songs of the Blind*), is published in Mexico.

1967   *Zona Sagrada* ("Sacred Zone"), his seventh book, fifth novel, is published in Mexico City; it is an undistinguished work and has received little attention. In March of this year his manuscript for *Cambio de piel* won the Seix Barral Prize in Barcelona, but Spanish government censorship prevented its publication there; it was published later in the year in Mexico, his sixth novel, eighth book. At the end of the same year it was published in English in New York with the title, *A Change of Skin*; an exciting work, in which he successfully fuses his "experimental" style with the fantasy/reality theme that fascinates him.

CHAPTER 1

The Historical Background

WE have said in the Preface that the formation of Carlos Fuentes is to be found in the period in which he grew up, both in Mexico and abroad. As a matter of fact, his childhood was very much like that of many children of cultured and cosmopolitan families in Mexico—divided between his homeland and the countries to which his father's interests carried him. In 1928, the year of Fuentes' birth, Mexico had barely settled down after a long period of revolutionary activity. So, the period of his early childhood—say the first seven years—is conditioned by the history which had preceded it and which had formed the society that he inhabited. In 1935 that society was still very uncertain of itself and would remain so until 1938, the year of the great oil expropriations by President Cárdenas. Therefore, to understand the environment that produced Fuentes, we must review some of the national history that went into making up the society of those years.

The three decades between 1910 and 1940 were years of crisis in the culture and civilization of Mexico, a time of decision and reappraisal destined to have profound and continuing effects. As a result, every aspect of the national life, including the entire aesthetic production of the period, was transformed. The era opened with a political revolution that was for Mexico a cataclysm as significant in its totality as were the revolutions of France and Russia. But this was only the first phase of a general social upheaval that in thirty years changed the face of the nation. As a matter of fact, the political revolution, which comprised the first seven years of the the crisis, may well have been the least important part of the entire period.

I   *Definition of "Revolution"*

In view of the total transformation in the political, social, economic, and cultural activities of the nation during this thirty-year period, it is evident that we must widen our definition of "revolution" and not limit our interpretation to the civil war that went on from 1910 to 1917. We must think of the Mexican Revolution as a total and continuing development, as a progressive maturation, on a national scale and in all fields of national cultural expression. This concept as applied to the political activities of the period is not a new one—it is implicit in the present name of the dominant political party, the *Partido Revolucionario Institucional*. The spokesmen of this party regard the revolution as a continuing process, no longer having to fight to maintain itself, but mature, institutional, and progressive.

It was a new idea, however, when applied to the whole cultural life of the nation. Romanell suggests it in his book, *The Making of the Mexican Mind;* Gaos and Ramos state it on the philosophical level; Vasconcelos had some idea of it in the 1920's. Another scholar, Paul Rogers, has said:

The culture of contemporary Mexico grew out of the strife and turmoil of the revolution. The year 1910 is as important in the development of the country's literature as it is in its political and economic history.[1]

It might be preferable to say that they are interdependent, neither growing out of the other, really—the strife and turmoil and the culture all coexisting and affecting each other in direction and results. The ideology must have come first, since no political revolution starts without men to start it, men who have been moved by powerful ideas in conflict with the official thought in force at the time. And in fact so it was, as we shall see below.

The strife and turmoil that began in 1910 as a political protest ended with the close of Lázaro Cárdenas' administration in 1940 as an institutional program. By 1917 the new and socially controversial Constitution, the result of seven years of ferment, had been promulgated (and denounced). And it was not until 1938, with the nationalization of the oil industry, that the revolutionary

goals were carried to their logical conclusion. This act of nationalization was, finally, the declaration of economic (and, on a
deeper level, psychological) independence—the culmination of a
conflict that had begun as far back as 1810 with the declaration of
political independence from Spain. It was the final triumph of the
ideology formulated in 1910 by the *Ateneo de la Juventud.*[2]

To understand the reasons for the deluge that swept before it
not only Porfirio Díaz and his regime but all that that regime
stood for, one must remember Juárez and the era of the Reform,
remember Morelos and the program proposed at Chilpancingo
in 1813, recall colonial times and the introduction of certain
Spanish political customs by viceroys such as Mendoza and
Bucareli, and try to understand some of the virulence of the
struggle. Nations, like men, cannot be understood without a
knowledge of their antecedents, their defeats, their triumphs.
Miguel Alessio Robles oversimplifies when he says:

When the dictates of public opinion are ignored, when government is
not in accord with law and justice, when the fundamental principles
of human liberty are trampled on, then we will see toppled the oldest
and most high-born dynasties and powers.[3]

This is satisfactory only if we see revolution as a simple revolt,
ascribable to the just anger of a betrayed people. This is not
enough if for only psychological reasons, to say nothing of the
philosophical probability that historic changes are the result of
the struggle and triumph first of revolutionary ideologies—we
need only think of the contribution of the Encyclopedists and the
philosophers of the Enlightenment to the French Revolution.

II *Political Factors*

It is usual to begin the political history of the revolution in
Mexico with the publication in 1909 of *La Sucesión Presidencial
en 1910* by Francisco Madero, and it was here that the ideological basis of the subsequent action was expounded. It can be reduced to a simple slogan: No Reelection. To understand the impact of that slogan, however, it must be recalled that Porfirio

Díaz, the dictator against whom it was hurled, had himself come
into office in 1876 on the same platform. He was ejected from
office thirty-five years later because of his cynical disregard of
that slogan. Also the slogan, No Reelection, is more than a mere
slogan. It has profound roots in the political consciousness of
the Mexican people, for they have learned by bitter experience
that one of the causes of constant uprisings and civil disorders
is the personal ambition of military "heroes" who are ever ready
to "save" the country and, once having done so, demand that
the country in turn show its gratitude by repeatedly reelecting
them to its highest office. Recalling Díaz, to say nothing of Santa
Anna, the Mexicans have carefully written into their Constitution that a military man must resign his commission before he
may run for office, and that a president is limited to one term in
the National Palace.

Madero was not the only ideologue to make himself heard.
Wide-spread opposition to any further reelection of the octo-
genarian dictator at once manifested itself. The Flores Magón
brothers (especially Ricardo), with their writings and speeches,
hastened to aid all incipient revolt, particularly in the factory
towns. Native newspapermen, like Filomeno Mata, who had never
been granted interviews by the dictator and his snobbish clique,
wrote fiery denunciations in subversive little journals. Another
group, quasi-official, and hence better organized, supported the
candidacy of General Bernardo Reyes to the vice-presidency.[4]
The country was electrified—the Creelman interview, the massacre
of strikers in Río Blanco the year before (1907), the internal
quarrels among the *científicos,* the growing unrest of the middle
class and even of the landowners—all foreshadowed the end of a
senile regime.[5] Charles G. Cumberland analyzes it so:

Many of those who turned against the Díaz administration, or who no
longer supported it, did so because they detected weakness. . . rather
than because they opposed the principles upon which he acted. These
men, including many of the great hacendados and financiers, were
quite willing to see Díaz removed from office, even though they
looked with horror upon fundamental changes in the government or
social structure. They were the men who made possible a successful
revolution against Díaz, but at the same time their attitude would
make it difficult for a reform government to function.[6]

III *Why Fuentes Is a Product of the Revolution*

The class theory of history, whatever shortcomings it may have, does point up similarities and parallel developments within the social levels. Carlos Fuentes, for example, has had the childhood and upbringing typical of the scion of a diplomatic family of the upper bourgeoisie in the 1930's. And Francisco Madero, the son of a rich landowning family, conservative and traditionalist, had the upbringing typical of his class. He was educated at home by the Jesuits, then in the United States and in France, where he spent six years, from 1889 to 1895. In France he had become a Spiritualist, and the theosophical ideas of this sect, plus his original humanitarian and idealistic impulses, made a reformer out of him. On one of his father's estates he had successfully experimented with a cooperative and he was convinced that the country's woes could be cured by education.

At first, it is true, he had shared some of the inertia characteristic of the well-to-do so long as they do not see their way of life menaced nor feel the need to help a neighbor, especially one who is of a different social level. This inertia, which was typical of his class in Mexico, was in some cases the result of resignation before the entrenched immobility of the Díaz regime; in others it was probably due to ignorance of the truly appalling conditions among the lowest classes. But Madero was not greedy, he was not ignorant, and he was more aware of the social injustices that swamped the country than were his fellow ranchowners. When he realized fully the vicious character of the political crimes of the central government, he pronounced for liberty and proposed to dedicate his well-being, his wealth, and his life to the service of the nation. He survived only until February, 1913.

It is not suggested that Carlos Fuentes is the same type of man—each of us reacts to similar conditions in his own way— but his background does show similarities to those of Madero. Fuentes also was educated at home and abroad. Exposed to the ideological winds of his time, he became a "fellow-traveller," and ardent desire for social justice finally in the 1950's led him to the Communist Party. In the 1940's many of his contemporaries, he among them, were cynically convinced that the Revolution was a failure. This attitude was largely a reflection of the disillusion-

ment felt by his parents' generation, which had been embittered
by the defeat of José Vasconcelos in the presidential campaign
of 1924. Eventually, at the end of the 1950's, Fuentes was to experience that further disillusionment that many intellectuals suffer when they find themselves squeezed into the doctrinaire
straitjacket by the Party. (He now calls himself a Marxist.) Survival requires compromise; Madero did not survive, Carlos
Fuentes has.

IV *Impact of the Revolution on Writers*

The story of the plot against Madero calls for the pen of a major novelist. It is a tale of ambition, betrayal, and skullduggery
in high places worthy of the Thane of Glamis. But none of
Mexico's major novelists since the Revolution has made it the
central theme of any of his works. Mariano Azuela would have
presented it as simply the crowning symptom of social cancer;
his concern was with the little people; it was not in his style.
Martín Luis Guzmán was far too preoccupied with his hero,
Pancho Villa, to see Madero as more than an inevitable casualty
in the progress of the Revolution. José Rubén Romero was too
much the humorist, he could not have adapted his pen to such
high and sombre tragedy. Agustín Yáñez preferred to show the
impact of the Revolution on the people of a small town, not on
those of the capital. Fuentes' *Artemio Cruz* would have no justi-
fiable place for such an episode within the stylistic framework of
its plot. Perhaps Rodolfo Usigli, who has so well dramatized the
Carlota-Maximilian tragedy, will some day be tempted to present
the drama of the death of President Madero. Perhaps there are
deeper psychological reasons for what is evidently a shying-away
from this event on the part of Mexico's artists. Perhaps they feel
it is too revealing, too condemnatory of the character of Mexico
itself—it arouses the same uneasiness that the assassination of
President Kennedy evokes in the United States today. Whatever
the reasons, it has had a deep effect on the following generations and may very well account for the despair felt by many intellectuals in the decade between 1924 and 1934. After all, Madero had been an intellectual. His murder was looked upon by his

class (whether correctly or not does not matter) as a rejection of sanity and order in the Revolution and as an open invitation to yet more violence and more betrayal. The tragic interval merits closer examination, for the principals have become prototypes for many stock characters in the literature of Mexico, and the basic motivations of the men involved in the tragedy have been transferred to their fictional descendants, almost to the point of becoming stereotypes. But the history of the conspiracies against the new president (Madero became president in the fall of 1911), and particularly against all his government implied, must be read in the history books since the scope of this essay cannot permit such amplitude.[7]

The net effect of the uprising against Madero and his assassination was to dispel all possibilities that the new "federal" government of Victoriano de la Huerta would be accepted by the country. What had begun as a revolution to overthrow Díaz now became a civil war. The whirlwind of vengeance stirred up by the overthrow of the first popular government in over thirty years gathered force in the great ranches of the North, and from Coahuila, Chihuahua, and Sonora swept down to avenge Madero and the ideals of constitutionality.

Governor Venustiano Carranza, the first to rise against the unholy team loose in the capital, took charge of the growing Constitutionalist forces. His army was soon strengthened by the addition of a much more formidable group led by such men as Alvaro Obregón, Adolfo de la Huerta (no relation to Victoriano), Plutarco Elías Calles, and others. And during the summer of 1913, the formidable Pancho Villa also recognized Carranza as First Chief and assembled an army of his "golden shirts" to fight in the common cause.

It is not necessary to follow in detail the ebb and flow of the war during the two years that followed. As was to be expected, there were many betrayals, clashes of personalities, injustices. In the eyes of the general public, the Constitutionalists were shortly as bad as the Federalists—who could take time to distinguish between *carrancista* or *huertista* bullets, or whether the marauding soldiers wore a federal kepi or a golden shirt.[8] And in April of 1914, President Woodrow Wilson sent American troops to Veracruz in an ill-advised attempt to aid Carranza indirectly.

Carranza, of course, repudiated this further intervention by the Yankees in Mexico's internal affairs, and in August he entered the capital victorious. During the course of the campaign, Carranza and Villa had quarreled bitterly and it was eventually necessary for Obregón (who at this time still supported Carranza) to subdue Villa in 1915 at Celaya. Zapata was not eliminated until 1919, and finally even Carranza himself was disposed of (in 1920). Obregón emerged as the "strong man" and was elected president. The war-phase of the Revolution was over and it could now begin to take institutional form.

V The Involvement of the Intellectual

Many men of letters were involved in these fluctuating fortunes of war, some being adherents of one party, others of another, and to us now their impressions are more interesting than the military and political game of seesaw.[9] They observed and recorded what they saw of the ambitious and unscrupulous men whose personalities and conflicts influenced the history of the country so profoundly. Carranza, Obregón, Villa, Calles, in particular, fascinated these writers, so that we have authentic first-hand accounts of what they were like. And these accounts in turn have influenced the subsequent generation of writers, amongst them Fuentes, who have been formed not only by the society that came out of the war but by the vision of it of all those artists who presented it inevitably, strongly, from their own point of view.[10]

So not only was it a period of political transition, but of total cultural change. The Díaz era had been gaslit, like the Victorian age in England, one of ordered leisure for the "decent" people. But as, with the Revolution, the material aspects of society were changing, so the philosophical ideas of the previous generation were no longer acceptable either. The Positivism of Gabino Barreda, which had been the semiofficial apology of the Díaz regime, was now just as discredited as the economic theories of the *científicos*. Justo Sierra himself had opened the way for the coming attack when he stated, in a public lecture in 1908, that it was possible to doubt the so-called scientific concepts of Positivism;

and two years later he actually supported by his presence the series of lectures offered by the *Ateneo de la Juventud.*[11]

This group spearheaded what was to be known as the Centenary Generation and their ideas were derived chiefly from contemporary French thought, especially that of Poincaré, Carnot, and Bergson.[12] The concepts of creative evolution and *élan vital* of the latter appealed particularly to Vasconcelos (whom Madero considered a fellow Spiritualist[13]).

Needless to say, the work of the *Ateneo* did not, could not, have any immediate effect on the social climate on a national scale. The time was not propitious to a general rebirth in the country's intellectual life parallel to that beginning in the political sphere, and after Madero's death the new leaders of the Revolution were much more men of action than of thought. Madero himself was certainly an intellectual and would have aided the work of the *Ateneo,* as is shown by the support he gave to the founding, in December 1912, of the first *Universidad Popular,* dedicated to the free education of adults.

While the work of the *Ateneo* may not have had any immediate effect on the Revolution, the close connection between the two is clear in the sense that they are both dedicated to freedom—one implemented the other—freedom for the expression of revolutionary ideas as well as of revolutionary actions, and their profound and far-reaching effects are still being felt throughout the whole Hemisphere. The work of the *Ateneo* was as much a part of the Revolution as were the battles "insofar as we take the Revolution to signify a *discovery* of Mexico *by* Mexicans as well as a *recovery* of Mexico *for* Mexicans."[14]

VI Summation

In reviewing the intellectual bases of the struggle, we must not for a moment forget the actual physical strain of the struggle itself. There was little time in those hectic days for philosophizing or for the elaboration of formal ideologies. Years of constant warfare had their effect on the inhabitants of the capital as well as on the rural population, and acute urban observers, to whom these revolutionaries were all bandits and scoundrels, have left us some sarcastic descriptions of the various conquering generals and their men.[15] Before going on to consider, in the next chapter, the socio-cultural results of all these various currents—which are now beginning to run together—it would be well to recall that the aesthetic productivity does not begin to flow strongly until after 1920, since to produce works of art, the rifle and the grenade must be set aside and the hand left free to take up pen or palette. The only form of artistic expression that is fully evident before that date is a popular form, the *corridos* or ballads, a sort of spontaneous folk-poetry, which rose from the heart and lips of a land in upheaval.

One word about the new Constitution of 1917, several of the more famous Articles of which have provided themes for subsequent literary treatment.[16] Article 27, for example, recognized the right of the villages and other communities to own *ejidos* (communal farm plots) and water; and Article 123 sought to protect the workers within the capitalistic-industrial system by providing for an eight-hour day, minimum wages, no child labor, no "company stores," plus other similar "progressive" legislation. In other Articles, "No Reelection" was emphasized; and, most importantly, national ownership of subsoil deposits was made an official dogma.

This brief historical panorama has provided, it is hoped, sufficient background to explain the formation of the next two generations of Mexicans. The period just summarized, a span of ten years, was one of destruction until 1915 (the defeat of Villa), and of consolidation until 1920 (the election of Obregón). Now it will be one of rebirth, of flowering, of institutionalization.

CHAPTER 2

Socio-Cultural Background

I *The Importance of Cultural Hybridism*

IT may be stated as a generalization (with rare exceptions—e.g., Rafael Landívar) that before the nineteenth century Mexican literature, as a cultural expression of the people, was not authentically Mexican. And it was rarely so even during the nineteenth century, although noticeable efforts were being made then towards establishing some sort of cultural independence. Before the nineteenth century, most literary efforts were unabashedly an imitation of Spanish or French modes. But during the nineteenth century, the cultural *mestizaje*—that hybrid quality so characteristic of a new nation—was evident in all manifestations of Mexican aesthetic expression. It was not until our own century, after the Revolution, that the inferiority complex that all such hybrid cultures begin by feeling was resolved and that Mexico could *accept* its *mestizaje* as a valid foundation upon which to build its own culture.

The roots of this hybridity in Mexican culture lie, to begin with, in the almost complete failure of the Spanish ruling caste, after the Conquest, to understand or to attempt to assimilate the culture of the peoples they had conquered. There were brilliant exceptions, of course, among the missionary friars. Even Cortés himself recognized that culturally the Mexicans were far beyond the level of the Caribbean Indians previously encountered. But by and large, the average Spaniard, conqueror or settler, was interested in ruling and exploiting rather than in understanding and assimilating. Consequently there were comparatively few attempts (again, with notable exceptions) to comprehend or preserve the formal manifestations of the indigenous civilization, such as the canals or the temples, so why would there be attempts to understand or preserve the more subtle poetic or aesthetic manifestations? And almost all the conquered ethnic groups, Mayans, Tarascans, Zapotecans, Nahuas, had an oral literature whose traditions, along with some specific examples, have come down to us.[1]

Thus the inevitable imposition by the conquerors of their own patterns on top of the flourishing civilizations of the indigenes could not help but produce a tremendous cultural confusion that could not even begin to be conceived of as resolvable until at least political independence was achieved. Indeed, until then there could not even be an attempt at definition as to what Mexican "culture" was. Not only was there a lack of definition as to what it was, there was even no agreement as to whether it existed at all. It was not until 1938—the year, as we have mentioned before, of economic *and* psychological independence—that a Mexican philosopher, Samuel Ramos, could ask whether such a national culture actually existed and undertook the task of trying to find an answer.[2]

However, Ramos did not begin with the aesthetic renaissance that began to be evident after 1920, perhaps because in 1938 it was still too close to be easily discernible. He preferred to approach the question from a philosophical point of view. Naturally, he was not the only one to begin to look for an answer to what was, after all, the paramount question. Other critics, too, tried to assess the meaning of the Revolution, although frequently they scarcely did more than reveal their own bias. If they were optimists, like Miguel Alessio Robles, they caught glimpses of a Golden Age:

Today, after the Revolution, one may note that mysterious effervescence that always follows great public upheavals, which after Plataea and Salamis gave the Hellenes the plays of Sophocles and the tragedies of Aeschylus; which after the tremendous agitations of the Roman Republic lit the vibrant inspiration of Vergil and Horace; and after the glorious battle of Lepanto called forth that magnificent chorus of writers and poets that awoke ancient Spain. . .[3]

This historian is allowing himself to be carried away somewhat by his own effervescence and is drawing high-flown comparisons. Yet it was concrete phenomena he was assessing, and the fact is that with no difficulty one may mention at least a score of talented men who in the short space of twenty-five years (from 1915 to 1940) produced a cultural contribution, in half a dozen different genres, that has enriched the cultural life not only of Mexico but that of the whole Spanish-speaking community of nations. Or, if they were pessimists, it was possible, at the very crest of the renaissance, to proclaim that "the Mexican Revolution is a failure. . . . its men are the same rascals as those of 1810."[4] In view of all this, then, it is quite time to ask, with Ramos, what *is* the culture that was forming and what are its characteristics?

II *Contemporary Mexican Culture*

As was mentioned above, the roots of this contemporary Mexican culture—as equally of any American culture—must be sought in the mixture produced by the imposition of a European mode on the indigenous. Bolívar himself, the best-educated and most intelligent of the Liberators, insisted that we of the Americas are by rights Europeans. And the Spanish culture imported with the Viceroys did not become Mexicanized during the first three centuries after the Conquest except indirectly and unintentionally. Of course, it could not have been completely Mexicanized, even deliberately, and that is why *indigenismo* (the cult of native patterns) can never be more than one among the many cultural currents that flow in the national life. The Mexicans themselves were certainly no longer Aztecs. But neither, despite Bolívar, were they Europeans. Therefore the intent, during the nineteenth century, to perpetuate, after the political independence, a neo-European culture became increasingly difficult and was bound to end in failure since it became constantly more artificial to try to imitate servilely or even by adaptation something that was not ours.

During the first few decades of the nineteenth century, however, it would have been equally impossible to develop a national Mexican culture simply because the Mexican nation as such had barely become a political entity. First of all, freedom from a sort of professional *criollismo* (insistence on Peninsular roots), as exemplified by Iturbide and Santa Anna, had to be won, and it was not until the era of the Reform that a start at the formation of a national Mexican culture could be made. The country was on the horns of a cultural dilemma: Mexicans were no longer Indians, but neither were they Europeans, so what was their culture? Except for the brief years of the Reform (approximately fifteen years, between 1857 and 1875, discounting the three-year Maximilian interval), the leaders and ruling classes did little to contribute to this formation. What had begun as a matter of policy and self-preservation for the Spanish conquerors and colonizers, a policy that attempted to deny the Indian culture and impose the European, solidified with the passing of centuries into an attitude, and persisted as an error long after the original reasons justifying it had vanished.

As the nation came into being and began to mature, this erroneous attitude became all the more artificial, tragic, and impossible. That was during the nineteenth century. For a few years during the twentieth (from 1920 to 1935, say) it seemed as though the opposite error—that of denying the European culture in order to reimpose the Indian—was about to be officially enshrined. Such an attitude was equally artificial and impossible. Neither the national nor the individual whim can contravene the heritage of history, or its own structure and circumstances. The historical factors necessarily determine the direction cultural development must take, and we can ascertain this direction only by taking into account all the factors contributing to the total life of the nation.

The double heritage, then, must be fully accepted, and the contribution of both the Spanish-European *and* the Indian ancestor must be reconciled. It is equally dangerous to insist that one is better or more important than the other. The result of such recalcitrance is (and had been until 1938) a sort of cultural schizophrenia. The typical cultured Mexican (and we must always bear in mind that we are talking about Fuentes) has been split in his inner allegiance. This may well explain why there has been so much public and private turmoil in the country in the years prior to 1938. It is a condition that has been tacitly recognized by most of the recent intellectuals. Manuel Gutiérrez Nájera, one of the most European of Mexican poets, was saddened by this inner conflict that seemed impossible to resolve. A split personality on a national scale is naturally evident not only on the cultural level. It was a rare and happy citizen who could accept himself as he was without trying to be or pretending to be something else. And unquestionably the conflict showed itself most acutely in that group that was the ethnic result of the two cultures: the *mestizo*, men partly Indian, partly European. As the *mestizo* class increased—it is now about 70% to 75% of the population—the urgency for a solution to the conflict similarly increased.[5]

If statistics mean anything, it is clear that the future of the nation must lie with the *mestizos*. The Indian as such cannot compete on a cultural level with the dominant neo-European civilization; and the cultural colonialism of the creole (a "white" Mexican of unmixed European descent) is almost completely discredited. Only the *mestizo* group, combining both heritages, can be the progenitor of a truly Mexican culture. This is a new role for a relatively new class. As late as 1910 it constituted only about 40% of the nation (with approximately 8% creole and 52% Indian) and in the nineteenth century it scarcely existed outside the big cities. All during the Díaz regime it was natural that this class, where it had any consciousness of itself as a class, should suffer, due to its mixed blood, a deep sense of social inferiority. So it was this combination of cultural schizophrenia and sense of social inferiority that the *mestizos* had to lose before they could take their place on a national scale as the natural source of contemporary Mexican culture. Since the Revolution they have increasingly done so and are continuing to do so.

III *The Fusion of Cultural Factors*

As a result of the total Revolution we have been talking about, a real fusion of the two principal cultural heritages was now possible between 1915 and 1940. The score or so of writers and artists mentioned previously were all *mestizos* and all (even Diego Rivera, who espoused *indigenismo* in its most virulent form) produced works of cultural *mestizaje*. Works, that is, in which the European (techniques, approach) and the Indian (themes, point of view) fused and produced a work of art. The Revolution accomplished all this first on the ideological-political level by breaking the old neo-colonialist way of thinking; then on a cultural level through those men whose work was a fusion of the two heritages; and finally on a psychological level, by President Cárdenas when he defied in 1938 the last bastion of neo-colonial exploitation. With his administration (1934-1940), a new coming-of-age (economic as well as psychological) produced an atmosphere propitious to the flowering of new attitudes and with them, out of the fires of Revolution, has come a new Mexican culture.

There are many other elements, of course, that have gone into the makeup of the new *mestizo* and his culture. Even though we have placed most emphasis, rightly, we believe, on the two most obviously important, it might be well, in passing, at least to mention two or three of the others, since all, after all, have gone into the formation of the new Mexicans (of which Carlos Fuentes is also part). *Indigenismo,* which has already been mentioned, influenced the work chiefly of Diego Rivera, José Clemente Orozco, Alfaro Siqueiros—all painters—and through them a vast number of other artists. The importance of the religious element, and the conflict between the supporters of the traditional Catholicism and the official new state orientation, can scarcely be underestimated. Indeed Ramos declares categorically that "all culture is always built on a religious sense of life . . . this feeling is the energetic source that feeds the creative effort."[6] To destroy the temporal power of the Church, as Calles did, does not destroy religiosity as an elemental factor in the national culture. And an important additional element in the new Mexican attitude is what may be called the "epic" sense of life. It may be tragic, or romantic and rebellious, or vital and optimistic, but it is there. The sense that Mexico has come of age and has a destiny which is finally in the hands of the Mexicans themselves, this is a difficult feeling to pinpoint, but it is there and is not to be frustrated any longer. Finally, even the mimetism of the nineteenth century cannot be considered as wholly a negative factor in the formation of the new Mexican character. In an inverted sort of way, it is a manifestation of individualism, and even the most original of artists must start his self-expression on a mimetic level.

To sum up, considering all these elements in the new national character, complementary, contradictory, it is hardly surprising that the fusion should at first have produced confusion, since all are essential to the new *mestizo*. The attempt to suppress, inhibit, some or any of them produced all the psychological difficulties he at first encountered in developing his own new culture; psychological difficulties such as the two already mentioned, a cultural schizophrenia and a feeling of inferiority, a self-denigration before the "superior white" culture (an "inferiority" that he overcompensated for in part by an exaggerated *machismo*), a psychological lack of self-confidence (that produces the violent criminal on one level or the embezzler on another). The Revolution cleaned out many of the contradictions by removing the inhibitions and by making suppression no longer necessary. It was a stupendous catharsis that helped the Mexican to escape from the domination of those subconscious forces that stultified him in his attempts at self-expression.

It is not too optimistic to think that a new national prototype already exists. It was emergent precisely in the generation to which Carlos Fuentes belongs. He, just as much as any other Mexican of his time, is a result of this new *mestizo* culture, which had its gestation during the centuries between Cortés and Díaz, and which officially came of age under Cárdenas in 1938. This is the generation whose members have reached maturity in the new Mexico, and one need only look at them and their work to realize that they are quite different from their predecessors, even from their own parents—newer, stronger, surer of themselves. Mexicans at last.

IV *Epic Mexico*

To pinpoint perhaps a little more closely some of these generalizations, it might be worthwhile to look more closely at some of the manifestations of what this writer chooses to call the epic sense of life, particularly in the generation of writers and artists preceding that of Fuentes. This epic sense of life is pessimistic and tragic during the early years of the Revolution and even as late as 1936. Mariano Azuela saw the Revolution as a disintegrating force; Vasconcelos saw it first as an opportunity for social experiment, to practice his humanitarianism, and next as a personal

insult; Rafael Muñoz saw it as material for tales to be told with
clinical realism; Orozco saw it as a tragedy, a universal suffering
shared by humanity. But since 1940, the feeling is no longer the
same. Mexico as a whole seems to have become vital and optimistic, it seems to have realized its own nationhood, that it has
awakened and is on the march. This is an enormous change, from
a tragic to a heroic sense of life, almost an about-face, in the
sense that now the Mexican looks forward and upward rather than
backward and downward. He has shifted from pessimism to optimism. This shift can be adumbrated in some of Rivera's work,
and it is even more evident in the new architecture of such men
as Juan O'Gorman and Mario Pani. What produced this tremendous reorientation of attitude that came about between 1935 and
1940 was the integrity of President Lázaro Cárdenas.

V *Cárdenas and the Psychological Independence*

Cárdenas did more in the six years of his presidency (1934-
1940) to implement the goals of the Revolution than any other
man since Madero.[7] It is not within the scope of this study to
itemize the many important details of his program; it must suffice to sum up by saying that this program was based on two im-
ponderables: the energetic reestablishment of the ideals and aspirations of the Revolution (which reawakened in the Mexicans
the self-respect and hope lost under Calles), and the sympathy
that the Roosevelt administration in the United States showed
toward Mexico and her efforts to consolidate the Revolution. The
culmination of the whole program came with the expropriation
of the oil industries in March, 1938. The courage and the overwhelming importance of this act cannot be too strongly emphasized since it was truly a declaration of economic independence and was immediately recognized as such by the entire nation. And, even more, it soon became quite evident that economic
independence can only be the result of a decision to declare
psychological independence. By this act, the Mexicans at last
lost their international inferiority complex, that feeling of not
being at home in their own land, which had inhibited for so long
the formation of their own culture. It proved to the Mexican
that he finally dared to outface the feared and powerful foreigner

not only on the field of battle (where it was usually too late) but on the field of economic interest (where nowadays the battle is won). By putting his own economic house in order, at the real risk of yet another intervention, he showed himself capable henceforth of ordering his own affairs.

At first there were difficulties and doubts, of course, and for a year or so it was not clear whether Cárdenas' program would achieve the success essential to the survival of the nation or whether it would end in failure and bring the anarchy that would end the experiment. Fortunately, through a concatenation of events too complicated (and fortuitous) to analyze here, both at home and abroad, the experiment was brought to a happy and successful fruition, and Cárdenas has taken his place beside Juárez as a father of his country.

So, it must be against this political and economic background that the psychological transformation mentioned earlier is to be explained: the *mestizo,* instead of accepting any longer that denigration which European culture had imposed upon him, now accepted the fact of *being mestizo* without feeling inferior about it. And since the psychological conflict was now resolved, he could dedicate himself to developing his own life and his own culture in his own eclectic way.

And this is exactly what Carlos Fuentes and most of the writers and artists of his generation have in fact done. The mimetism of the nineteenth century has been transformed, in the crucible of history, into artistic freedom and adaptability. The two heritages are still in counterbalance, but that is itself the achievement—they are now in counterbalance and not in conflict—of the fusion of the two. In any nation united in goals and no longer split by inner conflict and civil war, the arts must be eclectic and cannot be separated from the rest of the national life. Any current that influences one will influence the other; the socialism of Cárdenas in politics becomes humanitarianism in social relationships; the *indigenismo* of Diego Rivera in painting becomes agrarian reforms in legislation, and so on, each effect appearing under a different aspect as the man and his point of view incline toward the social, the political, or the aesthetic.

CHAPTER 3

The Renaissance of the Novel

FROM what has been said in the first two chapters, it must now be apparent that contemporary Mexican literature is as *mestizo* as the culture of which it is a part, and for the same reasons. The double source—Indian and Spanish—from which it springs has now fused to produce a single literature, in which, however, the two influences may still be traced. It must be emphasized also that no matter how strong the Spanish superlayer may be, the indigenous substratum is still indefectibly the basic ground of the Mexican nation, despite all overlayers of Spanish, French or, more recently, Anglo-American influences. This hardy native element is the taproot of the national geneological tree and feeds all its cultural branches, especially those of literature, with their pseudo-European foliage, changing with the literary modes and seasons, producing now the leaves of Neo-Romanticism, now those of Surrealism, or any other "ism" that may strike the writer's fancy, since for the modern occidental novelist, eclecticism must be the keynote (the meaning of eclecticism in this context will be defined later).

I *The Literary Genesis of Fuentes*

The revolutionary generation that was the first to express itself —that of Mariano Azuela—was just as subject to the influence of all its predecessors as any other form of culture, and one might legitimately talk of the Baroque or Neo-Classical elements, for example, in Azuela's early work. But actually there is no need to examine so closely this background common to all educated Mexicans of whatever generation. One need go no further than the Independence (1810-1821), which is when that eclecticism, so typically and inevitably Mexican, inspired by the effort to be free of foreign and even creole influence, first began to manifest itself. Fernández de Lizardi, for example, combines realistic, picaresque, and moralizing elements in a very eclectic fashion— almost too eclectic to permit unity of style—in painting a satiric picture of the society of 1816, especially in two of his works, *El Periquillo Sarniento (The Itching Parrot)* and *Don Catrín de la Fachenda* (a play on words, a title which is at once a name and a description: *Mr. Dude de la Pretentiousness*).

We must, however, say a few words about the two or three main literary currents of the nineteenth century: Romanticism, Realism, *costumbrismo* (literary portrayal of local manners and customs). Romanticism in Mexico never achieved the undiluted "Gothic" quality of Gil y Carrasco in Spain or of Walter Scott in England, but shaded imperceptibly into *costumbrismo* and vice versa. To the extent that it was *costumbrista*, it was that much more authentically Mexican. Even the novels of Manuel Payno, although Romantic in style and method, were really little more than serialized adventure stories in the style of Bret Harte, and they do not sustain the Romantic thesis.[1] The literary work of Guillermo Prieto, also, though touched with Romanticism, is more authentically Mexican, especially in such inspired collections as the *Romancero nacional (Collection of National Ballads)* or the *Musa callejera (The Street Muse).*[2]

Realism, on the other hand, produced more good writing; and it may even be said that Mexican literature as such definitely begins with such men as Ignacio Altamirano, Rafael Delgado, López Portillo y Rojas, Federico Gamboa.[3] Since Realism must by definition interest itself in what is real, these writers drew their material from their immediate environment, not from some imaginary medieval source or far-away exotic locale. Because of its method (recording the daily reality), they also had to concentrate on what was Mexican and not on what was Spanish-European.

One does not mean by this to indict Romanticism or to say that it served no useful purpose. The importation into Mexico of Romantic ideals, rebellious and democratic, paved the way for an acceptance of Realism as such. In turn, this permitted the transition to modern modes, some of which are still difficult to classify. Several of Azuela's so-called "Cubistic" works, such as *La Malhora* (the nickname of the female protagonist, roughly translatable as *The Unfortunate One*) or *La Luciérnaga (The Firefly)*, whose influence can be seen in some of Carlos Fuentes' stylistic experiments, still show *costumbrista* elements alongside the obvious Realism and Symbolism.

It is precisely because of these developments during the nineteenth century that the novel, of all the literary genres, was in the most adventageous position to adapt itself to the new needs of revolutionary expression evoked by the revolutionary events of the twentieth century. And since it was at this advantageous stage of development, it became the first genre to produce works that were of revolutionary orientation.

The rejection of native themes, a rejection that was implicit in the social philosophy of the Díaz regime, also was modified by Realism. And as soon as the fighting ceased and peace was restored, *indigenismo* developed in turn, passing through various stages, until it became almost officially enthroned during the Calles presidency (1924-1928). But if the Revolution has been understood for what it was—a social as well as a political and military cataclysm—then the extremes to which the literary position was carried will also be understood. The particular current known as *indigenismo* is being used only as an example and does not mean to convey that there were not other literary currents of great importance, such as *hispanismo* or *estridentismo*.[4]

II *Important Novelists of the Revolution*

The first writer to express the meaning of the Revolution was Mariano Azuela (1873-1952), and he was also the first of the new generation of writers who would carry Realism to its logical extreme and describe to us the real Mexico with all its problems: civil war, hunger, agrarian injustice, industrial struggles, political corruption, *caciquismo* (political bossism)—in short, all that is implicit in the social sense of the phrase "coming of age." The novelists of the previous century, even the Realists, had watered their work down with an excess of *costumbrista* material and this tendency had reduced the novel to a tedious formula, a combination of *costumbrismo* and moralizing. Lest this seem to contradict what was said earlier about the value of *costumbrismo*, let its different applications be considered: what was a virtue in Romanticism, because it saved the novelist from losing all contact with reality, could be a defect in Realism because it allowed the novelist to avoid depicting the unpleasant aspects of reality.

Azuela was a true pioneer in the contemporary Mexican novel, a revolutionary in literature as in life, and he reacted violently against the old formulas and eliminated many conventional devices such as plot, hero, love intrigue, etc., in order to go directly to dramatic reality as it was (or, at least, as he saw it). From this, as Manuel Perdo González points out,

> . . . is born a novel that is somewhat improvised, artless, but also without verbiage, rude and true to life, in which the central character may lack a name since he is the people, the anonymous mass . . .[5]

In the hands of writers less skillful than Azuela, this technique brought its own disadvantages: characters became mere symbols, narrative became skeletal, and the story a mere framework on which to hang social propaganda. This rarely happens with Azuela, whose mastery of simple prose style, authentic dialogue, and artistic sense of symmetry is as impressive in Spanish as is Hemingway's in English.

It is interesting to note that during this period (1920-1940), many works of different form will be offered (and accepted) as novels: memoirs, sketches, diaries, stories, "profiles"—almost all the prose produced by writers with any pretensions to style. It was new literature, revolutionary not only in theme but in form, and the old aesthetic canons were no longer applicable. F. Rand Morton's comments about the novel of the Revolution are most apropos:

> . . . the Novel of the Revolution is the external manifestation, sometimes plastic, sometimes spiritual, of the Revolution that changed the heart of Mexico. Hence, the Novel of the Revolution requires no plot, no style, not even well-defined protagonists. Neither does it require those literary mechanics that are usually taken for granted when one thinks of that arbitrary genre known as the novel. The novel of the Revolution requires only one thing: experience, be it personal, remem-

bered or imagined. Experience, that is, of an era during which a nation changed its whole way of thinking. If the Novel of the Revolution can recreate or portray this, its degree of technical perfection is unimportant . . . it fulfills its mission and fulfills the requirement of being a Novel of the Revolution. More than theme or style, plot or characters, it is the background that is important.[6]

In our consideration of the immediate novelistic antecedents of Carlos Fuentes, we begin with Azuela not only because he was the first to produce a "Novel of the Revolution" as such, but also because he was the first to recognize the great social upheaval as a source of inspiration.[7] In doing this, he was showing the penetration and concern he had always had in social matters. It was not something new for him as it was for other writers such as, let us say, Martín Luis Guzmán or José Vasconcelos. Azuela's choice of medicine as a profession, the practice of which he always considered more important than his literary work; his early activities in the political phase of the Revolution; his constant concern for the welfare of the "underdog"—all confirm this opinion.[8]

There were, of course, many other writers of interest who quickly followed the trail he blazed. Rafael Muñoz, Rojas González, Jorge Ferretis, Nellie Campobello, to mention only a few, are all inspired by some aspect or other of the cataclysm. Some describe the tragedy, others the social disorders, still others the confusion and exhaustion that followed in its wake. The literary activities of this whole generation of writers was most intense between the years 1925-1935 and it would not be unjust to say that the best work of the best novelists of the Revolution belongs to this period, but it would be wrong to think that after the last date no further work of value was produced. The Revolution, by then in institutional form, had an impact also in the sense that the new society with all its agitation and energetic commotion reflected the revolutionary ferment in all, not just the artistic, phases of life. Mexico awoke and bestirred herself with a gigantic shudder. It is unlikely that she will fall asleep again soon.

III *Azuela's Literary Attitudes*

It is worthwhile to examine Azuela's literary attitudes since, of all the writers of the Revolution, he has had perhaps more influence on subsequent generations than any other. His contempt and scorn for the intellectual of the middle class is balanced by his feeling—an implied feeling, since he never explicitly states it—that people of the lower classes are much more worthwhile, not in any Communistic "proletarian" sense, but simply that they are more interesting as material, as literary material. This is part of his diagnostic technique, which he carries into his treatment of all his characters. He was not only a doctor in real life; he was a doctor in his vision of society as well. His clinic, we are told, was open to all those who could not pay, and it must be recalled that the poor do not usually seek out a doctor until it is too late for preventive treatment. This is reflected in Azuela's attitude toward society as a whole. He is not so much interested in curing, it is too late for that, as he is in dissecting. The doctor is examining the corpse of society in order to discover the reasons for the disease. Similarly, Fuentes presents in *Artemio Cruz*, in the dying protagonist, the pathological symptoms of his physical and moral disease, itself symptomatic and symbolic of Mexican society. One might say of him, as Torres-Rioseco says of Azuela, that he "tries to perform a vivisection on his people, to show us their gangrenous viscera."[9]

To sum up Azuela's contribution, it is his profound comprehension of human motives and the insights that he gives to his readers, as much on the emotional as on the intellectual level, that makes him a great writer. He himself used to say that he wrote "only to unburden himself"; but actually, perhaps even unconsciously, his purpose was to perform the autopsy of Mexican society in order to reveal the necrosis that had set in and that, for him, had been produced by the Revolution. His clinician's eye saw all that was cancerous, gangrenous, disgusting and putrifying in it, but "he understood less the efforts toward national regeneration" that were to come out of it.[10] And this is the result of his having been first. For him the Revolution was a disillusioning, heartbreaking period of war between 1910 and 1917 followed by an equally heartbreaking and disillusioning struggle for power between 1917 and 1934. By the time the regeneration could really get under way, he had already done his best work, so that his vision of the total Revolution was never complete. He never saw beyond the evil that was produced. We must bear all this in mind when we note that his work taken as a whole seems to be a condemnation of the Revolution. His work, finally—and this is where Fuentes parts company with his influence—was an original and artistically vigorous defense of the dignity of man, which is what the implied ethical content of his position amounts to. His is the same tragic perspective of life that Orozco has (Orozco was ten years younger than Azuela), the same tragic sense of life that Unamuno felt in Europe at the end of a different era (Unamuno was nine years older). No matter what form their vision of life takes, these artists are pretty much of the same generation, products of the same world influences by and large, of the same *fin-de-siècle* disillusion. They are the inevitable "older generation," commenting on the disintegration of their society and, despite their great artistic penetration, unable to see cause for hope. That subsequent generations of artists would not have the same world view is most understandable; that they might or might not see cause for hope has nothing to do, of course, with the value of their work. Each generation interprets what it sees after its own manner. The potential for good or evil may vary very little, and if what is seen was, or now appears to be evil, then that is the particular artist's vision and his contribution. It is no less valuable and no less great art.

IV *Other Formative Novelists*

There are three principal formative novelists of the Revolution: Azuela was the first; the other two are Martín Luis Guzmán (1887-   ) and José Rubén Romero (1890-1952). Since neither Guzmán nor Romero had as much influence on Carlos Fuentes as did Azuela, we will not discuss their work so closely. Inescapably there is always contributory influence by all great artists of one generation (even in different genres) on those of the following generation. Very often not only the style or world outlook of a man makes up his subsequent influence, but his *method* as well may have great bearing on the way another later artist approaches the same problems in the new setting. Just as Azuela was a diagnostician (a method which was attractive to Fuentes for reasons we shall discuss later), so Guzmán was a judical analyst, his way of approaching a situation that of a lawyer confronted by a social condition that demanded analysis and explanation. Azuela saw the sickness of society and was disturbed by the futility of the suffering; Guzmán saw the injustices of society and was moved to analyze the reasons for them. Both reacted with pessimism to the Revolution, but whereas Azuela's pessimism was part of the heritage of his generation, Guzmán's was the result of disappointment in the leaders of the struggle, especially after the defeat in 1915 of the one leader that fascinated him. He had started off with a reserved and cautious optimism, but in *La sombra del caudillo (The Leader's Shadow)*, 1929, his disgust at Calles' *caciquismo* is evident and extends to that whole shoddy period of betrayals and opportunism. Azuela hoped, toward the end, that the social ills might be remedied by the cautery of Communism (although he was innately too pessimistic to rely too much on the "dictatorship of the proletariat"). Guzmán hoped that Mexico would turn in shame from the political gangsterism that was fastening itself upon her, and that is just what happened. And he himself, in the last twenty years, has returned to his original guarded optimism and has made a most successful adjustment to the new society and culture that have matured since 1940. Despite Azuela's Realism and so-called objectivity, we are forced to conclude that he is a much more emotional writer than Guzmán, much less intellectual. And this intellectual, analytical method is also part of Fuentes' personality as a writer and a great part of his life as a social being. His whole approach to politics is that of an intellectual (or had been up until 1960, when it is possible to see him beginning to turn his back on intellectualism as a method, and beginning to espouse intuition, Surrealism, even mystification, as preferable).

So it is chiefly Guzmán's analytical quality of mind, the clarity of his style, and his ability to capture a situation or a character in vivid unambiguous phrases that are the hallmarks of his prose. And we may say that Fuentes' perspective, his inquiring frame of mind, may be due in part, as were Guzmán's, to his many wanderings in Europe and the United States. Also we must not omit the consideration that Guzmán's work, perhaps because of its unclassifiable character, is most eclectic in its literary form, and this too is of great contributory influence on the development of Fuentes.

The influence on Fuentes of José Rubén Romero, the third of our great writers of the Revolution, is also indirect. It is Romero's attitude toward life, rather than his style or themes or method that influenced Fuentes. Although the theme of one of his most important novels, *Mi caballo, mi perro y mi rifle (My Horse, My Dog and My Rifle)*, 1936, is social injustice, both personal and governmental, as seen against the background of the Revolution, so social injustice is the prime motivator in many of Fuentes' literary reactions to his circumstances (in the Ortegan sense). Nevertheless, it is Fuentes' attitude toward the results of this social injustice which shows Romero's influence—the same ironic (but never wry) attitude toward life.

A word on the work of José Vasconcelos who, in his time (1882-1959), was one of the most controversial personalities in the intellectual life of Mexico during the first four decades of the present century. His influence is minimal, perhaps because his writing has been too personal and too irrational, in the sense that his intellectualism got in his own way. In a sense we might say he has had some influence on Fuentes, whose intellectualism has also occasionally got in his way, and whose Surrealism has bordered on the irrational. Sometimes it seems, to paraphrase Oscar Wilde's famous epigram about cynics, that an intellectual is one who knows the definition of everything and the meaning of nothing. And irrationalism as such is basically a Romantic pose. Vasconcelos was always a great Romantic, not only because of his political and amatory adventures but because of his philosophical rebelliousness towards life, his rampant individualism, and his fiery and vehement temperament. Fúentes, as we shall see later, also indulges in poses of various kinds and is on his way to becoming as much of a rampant individualist as Vasconcelos.

As Azuela was the first to give literary form to the Revolution, and as Guzmán was its chronicler and the portrayer of its most colorful personality, so Romero, who had no pretensions as a philosopher, offers in his outlook on life a non-moralistic approach which is evident in Fuentes' attitude toward life. Azuela, Guzmán, Romero—it is these three men who have contributed most to the native, Mexican development of Carlos Fuentes as a Mexican novelist. The intelligent and eclectic use he has made of elements of their style, their themes, their methods, their attitudes, will be touched on more specifically later. We have said enough to establish what was stated at the beginning of this chapter in connection with the *mestizo*, the eclectic and the revolutionary characteristics of contemporary Mexican literature. There are many other influences, foreign, European, Anglo-American, in the work of Carlos Fuentes, and they too will be mentioned later. Let us now attempt an evaluation of this formative period, formative chiefly because of the work of these writers here discussed, who were the direct progenitors of Carlos Fuentes and his work.

CHAPTER 4

Evaluation of the Formative Period

LET us evaluate what has been set forth and, we hope, established in the previous pages. It is evident, or should be by now, that Mexico has passed through several stages to reach her present position. Starting with a political revolution against a dictatorship, widening the aims to embrace ideals of social justice and of agrarian reform, fighting incipient native Fascism in the form of *caciquismo*, reacting against the totalitarianism implicit in Communism and the Regional Federation of Mexican Workers (*C.R.O.M.*), struggling to prevent the reimposition of militarism and personal rule, establishing the institutional Revolution, Mexico has emerged a strongly democratic nation with a developing culture of her own and a vital future.

Much still remains to be done, of course. There are and probably always will be, as in any living democracy, many continuing problems and perils to be met and overcome. The goals of the Revolution, the minimum objectives, were to satisfy the hunger for liberty and land, bread and justice. Political liberty first and then economic liberty have been attained. Like all young nations, Mexico had to learn, too, that liberty is not a synonym of license, and she learned this in the chaotic 1920's when the *C.R.O.M.* and the *Cristeros* between them showed what could happen if moderation did not replace extremism. With respect to the hunger for land and bread, satisfying one has satisfied the other, and in 1953 President Adolfo Ruiz Cortines was able to announce that Mexico had attained a long-sought goal: self-sufficiency in the production of food. This meant that the new class of small landholders (on the distributed lands), the village *ejidos* (communal lands), and the big cooperatives had reached a level of operating efficiency that the pessimists never thought possible, and this in turn implied an enormous job in education accomplished by the agricultural engineers and technicians, and by the *Banco Ejidal* in financing. And all of this gives the lie to those professional carpers who still cling to the old stereotype of the inefficient, bribe-taking Mexican and the incapacity of a *mestizo* people to rule itself.

As for social injustice, like the poor, it will always be with us in one form or another. There has been a tremendous gain on the positive side even though ideal conditions have not been achieved and probably never will be. There are still pockets of injustice, economic and social, in certain regions of the country and on certain levels of society, but with continued effort and good will the fight is being won. And Mexico has learned also that "the price of liberty is eternal vigilance." None more vigilant, or ready to scream high treason, than the intellectuals of the capital, naturally. Seek the most pessimistic picture of a nation's society and you will always find it in that nation's capital city, where the proximity to the trough almost inevitably makes everyone seem like pigs, where the inevitable "lobbyists" argue with sweet reason and long purse for their special interests. At one point in his career, Carlos Fuentes, an intellectual lobbyist of the Marxian utopia, saw social injustice everywhere; just as his reactionary counterpart sees a Communist behind every bush. We must not always accept the glib version of some facile pen when it depicts the decline of the West.

So these have been the goals of the Revolution. Now the problem is to guard the gains made and extend their benefits. For this the country needs an alert, honest, and responsible citizenry. To have such a citizenry a country needs a moral, honest, and preponderantly efficient government that will attract such citizens to its program and to its official ranks. Each is dependent upon the other, and this interdependence of social action is a part of democracy. The decisive turning point in the national life of Mexico came, as has been made clear, during Cárdenas' administration, between 1934 and 1940. The fact that the nation had at last an honest, just, upright, intelligent president, without unworthy personal ambitions, set an example that actually inspired a new standard in politicians and bureaucracy. We ought not underestimate the power of moral suasion when practiced by someone in the highest seat of power, and it was with this man and his administration that the whole direction of Mexican history since 1910 was confirmed. Luckily he did not, like Juárez, die before he could finish his work.

We have considered, too, what all this meant to the arts, to the culture of Mexico. And apart from all that has already been stated, it also meant a change of direction. Pessimism and the tragic sense of life could no longer be productive of universal works of art simply because there was no longer any need for such an interpretation.[1] Since culture is a product of society, it would seem that a nation produces works of art especially as a *result* of social turmoil—the artist feels the need to comment on what has happened around him. And one advantage that has come out of all the tragedy and waste of the Revolution is that most of the artists have felt the need to abandon forever their noncommitment, their aloofness from the social problems of their times. They have become aware of their own total role in society and their obligation to it: art for art's sake is no longer feasible. It is, on an individual level, the same thing that happened on a national scale—through an awareness of the need for social participation, the artist inevitably becomes more aware of himself too. He is no longer a social pet but rather a guardian and interpreter of culture. If he turns his back on this role and prefers to be or become a social pet, or some sort of dilettante, then he is abdicating as an artist and we must ask why.

I *The Importance of Indigenismo*

Before developing this last thought further, we must go back in order to go on. We must consider a bit more fully the importance of *indigenismo* in the development of contemporary literary directions. There was a period between 1925 and 1930 when the *indigenistas* intensively made common cause with the Communists, an uneasy collaboration which was bound sooner or later to be wrecked on the reefs of nationalism—the *indigenistas* were, of course, ultranationalistic whereas the Communists at that particular stage of their game were internationalistic.[2] Fortunately the old creole characteristics of indifference and inertia plus the Indian characteristics of impassivity and suspicion (especially toward those *indigenistas* who were not Indian) frustrated this attempt to impose an attitude just as erroneous as Hispanism or neocolonialism were. Many who point to Diego Rivera as the great apostle of *indigenismo* insist, with faulty logic, that if his artistic intuition was right then his ideology was also right, and thus justify not only *his* Communism but Communism in general. But there are many modifying factors which, if fully taken into account, make it most difficult to sustain such an oversimplification. We cannot enter into such a discussion here except to point out that Marxism as such was never a part of the official platform of the *Partido Nacional Revolucionario,* and that Mexican Communism never achieved anything like the monolithic quality of the Russian variety of that era. Even the controversial parts of the 1917 Constitution are no more than mildly socialistic legislation adapted to the specifically Mexican nature of the problems they proposed to solve. And as for justification, there is no great danger in admitting that historically Marxism served its purpose in Mexico by alerting the collective conscience of the community. There is no need to deny that by and large Mexican Communism helped and supported the program of the Revolution—*why* it did so is another matter.

The concomitant efforts of some painters and writers to revive Hispanism did serve to help revalidate the Spanish influence as of prime importance and also helped to counter the exaggerated *indigenismo* that proclaimed itself the only element in Mexican culture. In architecture, after 1940, the influence of the severe functionalism of the extremists was in turn modified by *indigenismo,* which sought to adapt Bauhaus dicta to local conditions and native needs. So the conscious, almost willful, combination of neo-European and *indigenista* elements was really the first attempt at producing a style that would be truly Mexican. Subsequent efforts were soon applied to other genres, and *indigenismo* and Hispanism—the two most important trends, still dominant, in the artistic expression of the new generation of Mexicans.[3]

At first, of course, it would not have been correct to equate *indigenismo* with nationalism. But as with the concept of revolution, so we must modify our standard definition of nationalism, that it may be understood in the Mexican context. López Velarde, the poet, understood this when he expressed the thought that even a new interpretation of patriotism would be needed, and he appealed to all that was noble in the hearts of his countrymen when he reminded them that *la patria es impecable y diamantina* (almost a metaphysical statement: "the motherland is immaculate and diamond-hard").[4]

The same sort of concept can be seen in the architecture of Obregón Santacilia and the music of Revueltas.[5] This was not nationalism in the ordinary chauvinistic sense of the word, which exaggerates the national importance for fear of being thought unimportant. It really was a new concept of patriotism and it was expressed aptly in one of the official slogans of the time: *En caso igual prefiera el producto nacional* (Given equal quality, choose the national product). Note the adjective "equal." It was not proposed that the national product be preferred simply because it was national. But at least there was a national product, and the slogan helped focus the collective awareness of a new national productivity. And so, little by little, the whole country began to be aware. The artists had seen it first—that through the fullness of what is national one reaches the universal, and that through the particular currents that contribute to a national culture one joins the general stream of world culture in the twentieth century, a century of perilous transitions, with an epic sense of life and destiny.

Without elaborating a whole racial, economic, historical, political, social theory around *indigenismo* in Mexico, for our purposes it is enough to recognize it as an effort to restore to the Indian his rightful importance as a primary cultural element in the national life.[6] This effort was deliberately fostered by those men who realized that the Indian is the common denominator of all the political, social, economic, educational (and other) problems that faced the new governing class, and that an attempt had to be made to solve these problems, his problems, if for no other reason than that the Indian constituted (at that time) about forty percent of the population. Vasconcelos showed deep recognition of this situation when he undertook his vast campaign in

1921 against the illiteracy of the sixty-six percent that did not know how to read or write. Thirty-four million pesos were set aside for this campaign in 1923, and by 1950 the average illiteracy had been reduced to thirty-seven percent.[7] Other aspects of the problem of the Indian were pointed up by the archeological and anthropological investigations that were organized to study and reevaluate the autochthonous cultures. It was inevitable that once all this aggregation of interests developed and was understood as a vital element in the culture of the nation as a whole, the policy became less one of assimilation and more one of acculturation (especially as the Indians themselves did not "cooperate" with the idea of assimilation).

Parenthetically, it should be made clear that *indigenismo* is not solely a Mexican phenomenon. It exists as well wherever the importance of the Indian is felt, due to his being a racial majority, in such other countries as Bolivia, Peru, Ecuador.

Of course, it was high time. The denigration of everything native during the dictatorship was one of the most arrant injustices of the Díaz regime, all the more shameless from a literary point of view since, of all the valid themes available to a Mexican writer, the Indian offered an inexhaustible source for authentic exploitation. Manuel Pedro González states it succinctly:

The indigenous mentality . . . with its terrible complexes, with its psychological, religious and social conflicts; with its theogonies, its magic rites, its legends and traditions; with its religious and cultural syncretism; with its intimate tragedies, its resentments, its emotional repressions, its spiritual personality [all] divided and wooed by two incompatible cultures and religions [its own and the Hispanic, of course], two forms of life and economy which are mutually exclusive and incompatible, constitutes a theme which is highly attractive to any creative fantasy that is able to penetrate into it with lively sympathy, divested of prejudices of class or culture.[8]

In spite of much official hypocrisy and the bored ineptitude of a bureaucracy that, like all bureaucracies, seems to congeal everything it touches, the efforts of the Revolution to integrate this basic and vital element of the national culture have permeated the social mass little by little and have been the leaven that has caused, is causing, and will continue to cause for a long time to come, the implementation of the Revolution.

II *Mestizo Equals Eclectic*

To be *mestizo*, as we have said, is to fuse, with equal acceptance, the Indian and the Spanish-European elements that equally contribute to the makeup of the national character. And to be Mexican is to be *mestizo*. When it is said that the artists knew all this first, the generalization must be qualified. Unfortunately not all artists and writers have known it, or have wished to accept it, and some have turned their backs on the idea of a *mestizo* culture, for one reason or another. Some of them, and a case may be made for including Fuentes, have not been able to adjust to, accept, comprehend, identify with, this new concept. Why? Perhaps because of being too international, too cosmopolitan, too rootless, too cynical, too "modern"—all these reasons are really the same thing: because they do not wish to be Mexican, since to be Mexican means an acceptance, wholehearted and uninhibited, of the fact of being a *mestizo*. Any rejection of such a fact must ultimately be based on some very personal reason in the artist's makeup. This may be a profound reason, some sort of psychological snobbism, perhaps, or it may be quite superficial—he won't play if he's not made commissar for cultural affairs. In any case, it usually involves not seeing that it is actually an advantage to be *mestizo*, since to be *mestizo* is to be eclectic (ethnically or culturally).

When Fuentes' first novel, *La región más transparente (Where the Air is Clear)* was published in 1958, someone said that it was to be translated into English and an unkind critic remarked, "I thought it had been translated from English."[9] Aside from the obvious implication, to a certain extent this catty observation was justified. There is no question that it is derivative—the influence of certain Anglo-American writers is all too evident, Faulkner, Dos Passos—but by the same token, what is not derivative? All young writers are derivative and Fuentes at that time was only thirty years old. Derivative is the road to eclectic, and it is a rare and vast talent indeed that need not travel it. What is eclecticism if it is not a choosing, a culling, a selection? Not at random, but a selection of what is thought best from various sources. It seems to appear when powerful or antagonistic forces are in the field, usually in an era of heightened historical awareness. Unlike syncretism, it does not modify for the sake of reconciling, rather it selects those diverse elements that are psychologically satisfying or felt to be necessary, and thus gains whatever consistency it may have from the inner integrity of the eclectic's own temperament.[10] All these conditions are present in mid-century Mexico, and to say that Carlos Fuentes is merely derivative is to be woefully incomplete. The German composer, Carl Werner Henze, paraphrasing Goethe, says that "an eclectic is one who, out of what surrounds him, out of what goes on about him, applies to himself that which conforms to his own nature."[11]

So, to be *mestizo* is to be eclectic. But to be eclectic does not mean being *mestizo*. One can be an eclectic writer in Mexico without being a Mexican writer, despite the accidents of birth or citizenship. And one may use Mexican ambiance, characters, background, simply because of proximity or geography, without necessarily partaking of them oneself. Leader of cliques, champion of the *nouvelle vague* (new wave) in the movies, polemicist, member of the international set, pet of foreign editors, cosmopolitan, intellectual—this is why Carlos Fuentes is eclectic, not because he is *mestizo*. To make the point quite clear, compare a writer like Fuentes with a writer like Juan Rulfo. The latter is truly Mexican in a sense that Fuentes will never be, nor would ever wish to be. Does this make Fuentes any the less a "good" writer? Not at all, it merely makes it more difficult to consider him a Mexican writer. The difficulty is easily eliminated if one assumes that it is unnecessary to consider him a Mexican writer. Simply judge him as a writer. Unfortunately, it is not quite that simple—he is a Mexican and a writer and somehow the two seem to be inextricably combined. So it has been necessary to show what being Mexican is before we can state with any persuasion that Fuentes is not, in the ordinary meaning of the phrase, essentially a Mexican writer.

It is a cliché to say that a writer is the product of his time and place, and it may even be a true statement about the great majority of writers, but what if a writer has no place or deliberately turns his back on his time? One cannot force an artist to fit a

Procrustean bed willy-nilly, and superficial categories are quite often inadequate when applied to such complex and talented individuals. Just as some writers are simpler than others, so some are more undecipherable than others and are not to be analyzed or classified by the simple application of copy-book maxims. And the matter becomes even more complicated if one considers (as one must) such dicta as that of Dr. Edmund Bergler, that all writers are driven by a compulsion neurosis. An ordinary critic cannot hope to offer a psychoanalytic evaluation, yet he must, to the best of his ability, try to take all these factors into consideration when making his judgment, if he wishes to be in any way adequate in his summation.

The very fact that a writer such as Fuentes can turn his back on his place while constantly using it as the locale of his books is most intriguing in itself. It makes one think that what happened in United States culture at the end of the nineteenth century—one need only mention Henry James—may be happening now in Mexican culture. The parallel is apt: if you say that Mark Twain is more an American writer than Henry James, then you can equally well say that Juan Rulfo is more a Mexican writer than Carlos Fuentes. When a writer deliberately chooses to live outside his own country, either one of two reasons is usually operative. Either his own country irritates him so that he can no longer work freely there (even for simple reasons of climate: Robert Graves lives in Mallorca because he cannot abide the physical climate of England); or he finds the foreign residence much more stimulating (for whatever reason). The reason is important, just as it is important to know why an eclectic artist selects what he selects. When we discuss the personal formation of Carlos Fuentes in Chapter 6, we will have occasion to inquire more closely into these criteria.

The Revolution and the Indian provided tremendous themes and an abundance of them for writers of two or even three generations, concurrent to and subsequent to the event itself. It provided tremendous settings and background for the working out of those themes. And just as the Revolution went through three discernible phases, that of outright war, (1910-1917), that of the struggle for political power (1920-1938), and that of institu-

tionalization (1938-   ), so the development of the three revolutionary generations of writers seems to have gone through an
analogous three stages: that of pessimism (Azuela's *Los de abajo*,
1915), that of struggle between *indigenismo* and Hispanism
(Gregorio López y Fuentes' *El indio*, 1935), and that of assimilation into the national consciousness of the completion of the
Revolution (Juan Rulfo's *Pedro Páramo*, 1955). It will be noticed
that Carlos Fuentes does not figure here.

These are the main considerations with which we must reckon
if we are to understand why some writers have accepted their
heritages and others have used it in spite of what is basically
a rejection of that same heritage. It is not to be understood that
Carlos Fuentes rejects the *material* of the indigenous, its myths,
its settings, all that Manuel Pedro González lists in the quotation
above; he makes very good use of it—but that is the point, he
uses it as a sort of exotic milieu, to give color and fascination to
his work, uses it as a foreign writer might (as Graham Greene
or Evelyn Waugh have done), not ever being part of it or allowing it to be part of him, not showing any identification with or
even acceptance of that part which is ineluctably his. All this is
most complicated and it is said neither in sorrow nor in condemnation but as a key to the personality and writing of the man, who
must be fully considered before either he or his writing can be
understood or placed in their proper perspective of time and
place.

CHAPTER 5

Recent Directions

THE involvement, mentioned in the previous chapter, of Mexican artists, their commitment to a total role in society and their obligation to comment on the social problems of the time was felt particularly strongly in the second generation of the novelists of the Revolution. In the third generation—that of Carlos Fuentes— we can already begin to discern a rejection of awareness, a rejection which now in the 1960's has almost assumed the proportions of a school. Also, as the Mexican artists approached the universal through their nationalism, by becoming less parochial in their vision, some have gone to the extreme of becoming cosmopolitan in all senses of the word except the humanistic. The dehumanization of the arts that Ortega detected as a world trend as far back as the 1920's has become in some advanced cases a dehumanization of the artist. The history of human development being what it is, it was inevitable that this should occur.

And since, from 1940 on, Mexico has become increasingly a participant—no longer isolated by the urgency of her own special problems—in the wider theatre of Occidental culture, we need no longer restrict our consideration to the specific milieu, or *circunstancias*, that, having produced the three generations discussed, now widens into the world stream. To the point, indeed, where the strong currents in Mexican literature, all quite individualistically discernible up to the 1940's, become in the 1950's and 1960's so placid as to inspire some critics to comment on the "decadence of the novel in Mexico."[1] What they are commenting on, really, is only an aspect of the decay of the novel in the West. There is some doubt indeed that the novel as a literary form has much further to go. Perhaps this is due to the fact that

some of these critics are still trying to define the "novel" in traditional terms. If nothing else, the twentieth century has obliged
us to reformulate many of our definitions—revolution, patriotism, art—now "the novel."

We have also said that works of art are the result of periods
of social turmoil, but social turmoil is usually a local condition;
since 1910, in both hemispheres, to have social turmoil on a large
geographic scale has meant world war. Since 1945 there has
indeed been the fear of such a global cataclysm—a third world
war. But in the last six or seven years this fear seems to have
died down, chiefly for two reasons. First, that no one can live in
constant fear all the time, it is too stultifying—even the hydrogen
bomb is no longer the bogey that it once was and can now be a
subject for jest; and second, that there has been a very real and
visible *détente* between the two great antagonists—neither wishes
to risk self-destruction in destroying the other. So that in speaking of the decadence of the novel in Mexico or elsewhere in the
West, one is merely observing a phenomenon of the times—that
we seem to have entered one of those historical eras of transition, out of which must come either a new synthesis, if mankind
is to survive, or a new holocaust, if it is not. The artists, like
everyone else, are waiting to see what happens. While they wait,
they continue to produce works that reflect the new world
climate.

I *Specific Trends*

One of the first trends to become apparent in the postwar generation of writers (and at this point we can merge the meaning
of "post-war," which can now equally well refer to post-revolu-
tionary in Mexico and post world war in the rest of the Occidental world) was that which has become known as *tremendismo*
in Spain and what Blanche Gelfant has called "the city novel" in
the literature of the English-speaking peoples.[2] Louis Ferdinand
Céline, the French novelist, was one of the first of this school,
with his *Voyage to the End of Night* (first English translation
published in 1934); and the trend was confirmed in the United
States with the short stories of Tennessee Williams and the novels
of Nelson Algren. Some critics went so far as to see it as a "post-

Naturalistic" school and gave it the subtitle of *Mystique de la Merde*.[3] It is a trend that depends to a great extent on shock for its effectiveness. But in a thoroughly shocking world, shock no longer has much effectiveness. In Mexico it is to be seen as early as 1935 in the work of Rafael Muñoz, who achieved great effect by combining brutal realism of style with impressionistic imagery of description. In writing of a battle, for example, he talks of a hill that burned like a "drunken volcano," and goes on to speak of the "star-spangled bereavement of the night."[4]

The cult of *tremendismo* is of course one of the first results of the extreme permissiveness in all fields, including the aesthetic, that became evident in the West as an aftermath of the great Depression and the Second World War and the cynicism and despair they engendered. There is, in this position, a great danger, one that an American critic, David Daiches, makes clear in connection with American literature by asking the question: Is the writer a serious artist or commercial?[5] Shock, in literature, has always been most salable, and after the war the floodgates opened. But the bourgeoisie has cooperated with such delight in the game of *épater* that we must now seek a new definition of "shock." At this point the critic, driven to the wall, throws up his hands and dismisses shock as a concept no longer meriting any artistic consideration.

Daiches' question about commercialism is one, however, that must be considered with attention, especially in the countries of the West, where the seductive power of the dollar, the general desire for *la dolce vita,* and the new hedonism in general (another new definition!) have proved to be a grave temptation even to artists and writers of considerable merit. Especially in countries where traditionally writers have enjoyed great prestige but little remuneration, they are eager to be noticed by United States publishers, eager for translation, eager for pressruns of fifty, a hundred thousand copies. This yielding to the fleshpots has been decried ever since Esau sold his birthright for a mess of pottage, so we need not be detained here by it except to note it further on as a factor in that process of selectivity mentioned before.

After *tremendismo,* after the impact of the wars has receded, after the floodgates have opened—what? One of the most important changes in the directions of the novel is, as a contemporary critic, Janet Winecoff, says ". . . in the area of novelistic theory."[6] Among the new practitioners in Spain (which, after all, has as much influence on Mexican writers as does France or the United States), who are trying to develop in their fashion within the larger framework of Occidental trends, are those known as the *objetivistas*. These "Objectivists" have developed what they choose to call the *novela nueva* which extends the development known in France as the *nouveau roman* by permitting, nay insisting, on social awareness as part of the concept. As Carlos Fuentes has assimilated many of the theories of the *nouveau roman* (to the extent, indeed, of turning his back not only on *indigenismo* but also on social involvement as such), we must look a little more closely at the theories developed by this group.

The Objectivist writer, in Spain, ". . . abstains from analysis, comment or interpretation . . . reserving these functions for the reader, who thereby participates in the creative process . . ."[7] In France, the theory does not include an insistence on social involvement—that has been a development of the Spanish Objectivists, due to their own particular *circunstancias*, and as Fuentes is more influenced by the French than by the Spanish group, he too has eschewed further social commitment. Fuentes has seen, quite logically, that any commitment, social or otherwise, would inevitably weaken the Objectivist position. Of course, he was not always so uninvolved. This has come about after his break with the Communist Party and the weakening, little by little, of his concern with social injustice. It so happens then, that the "purer" position of the French Objectivists also suits his own interest better. And all the Objectivists are agreed that the psychological novel is dead, or at least not fit for discussion amongst novelists who have any pretensions at being "contemporary." More will necessarily be said about this in our discussion of Fuentes' most recent work.

There is, of course, still another school of contemporary writers, neither *tremendistas* nor Objectivists, who are, as a matter of fact, looked down upon by the latter group as impossibly old-fashioned because they still try to "write novels." Since the ideal, at the moment, is *la literatura sin autor* (authorless literature), it is almost shameful, by this canon, to admit to any auctorial intervention at all.[8] One wonders how these authors can bear to have their names on the title page or accept royalities. But the other, more old-fashioned, group keeps right on writing novels as though its members did not realize that such a procedure is no longer possible. This "traditionalist" group is represented by such men as Luis Spota, Sergio Galindo, Rafael Solana in Mexico or Enrique Laguerre in Puerto Rico. They feel that they have something to say and that they can still do so in a more or less straight forward fashion; they have not, in other words, worried so much about theory as such. This is not to say that they have not been influenced by the same precursors as the others—Joyce, Faulkner, Céline, Azuela, Cela, and so on. They have simply been less preoccupied with their position as writers and more concerned with their actual writing. Laguerre has stated the attitude toward writing that might be called traditionalist and it is worthwhile to see what he says since even the Objectivists, despite their extreme theoretical position, do perform as authors and do produce literature.

II *Five Auctorial Bases*

Laguerre sums up the positions as follows.[9] There are five basic considerations upon which any writer must construct his work, no matter what his aesthetic rationalizations may be and whether he recognizes them or not. The first indispensable, essential consideration is the life experience of the writer. Of course, by "life experience," he means here *all*, the total, experience of the writer's existence, not just the outer, accidental "facts" of his life, but his inner, existential life as well—the total life product: personal, vicarious, collective, circumstantial (his contact with the outer world), imaginative, including all those aspects not named, unnameable, fragmentary, real, unreal, dreamt, fantasied, that go to make up an individual. Whether he is able, or even wishes, to draw upon this total source, depends on his purpose and his mastery of technique, or techniques (since there is no reason why he should limit himself to one). Laguerre rather thinks that the personal factor is enriched by taking a perspective towards it which he describes as "Magical Realism." This is a concept taken from the jargon of contemporary painting, which similarly holds to what has been stated above about the total reaction of the artist. It is also a definite technique which, in the hands of a good painter, produces a translucency and clarity that is lovely—it can be seen, for example, in the works of Salvador Dalí, who applies this technique to Surrealism. How this is to be transferred from the canvas to the printed page is not too clear; but in the hands of a master a similar effect is produced—Alejo Carpentier or Jorge Luis Borges come to mind.

The second basic consideration follows logically from the position outlined above—it is, in effect, the technical resources that the writer brings to his work. This would, one supposes, inevitably be conditioned by his basic aesthetic theory, his theoretical position vis-à-vis the novel as such. Perhaps that is why the Objectivists are not able (when they say they do not wish) to write in this fashion. In these novelistic techniques or resources figure such elementary stylistic devices as first-person presentation, epistolary style, stream-of-consciousness, Proustian associative writing, etc. In short, the true eclectic position—anything that produces the desired effect is acceptable.

Third among the basic considerations which must guide any writer is his ideology. This is not meant in the restrictive sense of political ideology. It must mean the total life outlook, the existential position, his *Weltanschauung,* and can include his "official" position as well—be he a Surrealist, a Symbolist, an Objectivist—whatever it may be. Of course it does include his political ideology as well, since we are dealing with a total individual here, and which aspect is preponderant will depend on the stage of development through which the author is passing at the moment, not just as an artist but as a human being.

Fourth among the basic considerations upon which a writer constructs his work is that of characterization. It may be objected that this is really a part of technique, a technical resource, but not as Laguerre means it. Characterization to him and the group for which we are using him as a spokesman is, next to life experience, the most important of all of the bases he talks about, and it is only incidentally a technical resource. Actually, it is the ability to characterize that is to be considered the technical resource, whereas characterization itself is much, much more—it combines with the life experience and with the ideological position to produce in the *personnae* of the work that particular translucency or clarity of presentation that is then defined as Magical Realism. In other words, it is this fourth element that synthesizes all the others into an artistic whole, and it goes far beyond the simple ideas of psychological consistency or trueness-to-life. As a matter of fact, the penetration implied by complete characterization may be psychologic, poetic, charismatic, Surrealist—anything but Objectivist—since for Laguerre Objectivism is an error, an impossibility; he feels that its own self-limiting definitions force it to be incomplete.

And fifth, the whole production must be invested with the "poetic atmosphere" (what we have previously called the "epic" sense). For a prose writer, this must not be too poetic, in the sense of rhythmic, for then he will no longer be a novelist but a poet—a fate which, in Laguerre's analysis, has indeed befallen such a writer as the Spanish stylist, Gabriel Miró. This consideration may also be broad enough to admit various definitions of reality, from the ultrareality of fantasy to the infrareality of *pointillisme* (which, in literature, is an excessive preoccupation with trifling details).

This elaboration of Laguerre's is by and large, one of the most concise and pointed statements about modern novelists that one could wish for, and it is possible to understand that even the Ojectivists, rejecting as they do all formal acceptance of such bases, are still bound by them since in the last analysis there is no such a thing as an "anti-writer" (in the same sense as there may be an anti-hero, or even an "anti-book") but a man cannot be at the same time a writer and a non-writer. Such an idea may be all very well for bandying about in some game of words (as Don Quijote *talks* about *la razon de la sinrazon* [the logic of unreason]), but no one can actually live it, since a thing and the negation of that thing cannot coexist in the one object at the same time.

Since the Objectivists have, to all intents and purposes, painted themselves into this logical corner, and some of them are sane enough to recognize the fact, one may ask, how do they justify, or insist upon maintaining, the theoretical stand they do maintain? Those who are sane enough (and let us not hesitate to say that some are not) to recognize the untenable quality of their position maintain it simply because the quixotic posture of maintaining an untenable position appeals to them. This is their contemporary way of shocking the bourgeois. Or perhaps it is simply the old artistic impatience, stated by Emerson and Whitman, with consistency and logic. In this particular case, consistency and logic are seen as bourgeois, and consequently as anathema, since all that is bourgeois, to the Objectivists, is *ipso facto* to be ruthlessly eliminated. It is naive to think, then, that Objectivism in the modern sense has anything to do with the old objectivity of the Realists, that simple obligation to present, in the phrase of the Spanish Naturalist, Emilia Pardo Bazán, *la dura verdad* (the harsh truth). Taken to its logical (or illogical) extreme, Objectivism is a total rejection of all previous formulations, prior certainly to the application of Marxism to literature, since "historically" (as the Marxists say), all literature has been "inexorably evolving toward *objetivismo,* which is the zenith of literary possibilities."[10] So, since Carlos Fuentes is an avowed Marxist, not now politically but aesthetically, he is therefore also an Objectivist. The implications are many and important. But, since a non-writer would have to be considered, in all justice, only by a non-critic, we must either abandon our attempt to write a critical essay on Fuentes and his work or else refuse to paint ourselves into the same corner by refusing to accept the non-logic of such a position. We prefer, obviously, the latter and will continue to talk of Carlos Fuentes as a writer, adopting for our purpose the statement made by Enrique Laguerre, and applying his norms to the works we will consider in subsequent chapters.

CHAPTER 6

Personal Formation

IN writing about the personal formation of a contemporary figure, one must try to steer the delicate course between the necessary and correct factual information on the one hand and the unnecessary possible indiscretion on the other. In the case of a man like Fuentes, such a course is difficult to steer since his whole life is almost inextricably involved with his work—the latter is very much the result of the former. This is no doubt true about any contemporary and makes it impossible to obey the New Critics in their insistence that we judge a work in and of itself: such heroic divorce of cause and effect amounts to a refusal to see a work as the product of a flesh-and-blood individual. A concomitant peril is that of being swayed, after long immersion in his works and association with his way of thinking, by the author's style towards unconsciously adopting his state of mind (morbid, impish, Olympian) and, almost without realizing it, finding oneself producing a parody of the subject (run-on sentences, mocking intellectualism). This chapter will try to avoid these perils and present only what seems necessary to as thorough an understanding as possible of the man *as a writer,* as a creative artist, and of his work.

In the first place, it must be kept constantly and firmly in mind that all the information, and much more, presented in the first five chapters of this study is intimate knowledge to Carlos Fuentes and has had tremendous formative influence on him as a man and as a writer—as an organism reacting to the environment (as Pío Baroja, Hemingway's *maestro,* put it in *El arbol de la ciencia [The Tree of Knowledge]*). Since Fuentes' creative production is part and parcel of that reaction, inevitably all this background "environment" has had an equally tremendous influence on the points of view he has at one time or another adopted, and even on the eventual attenuation as cosmopolitanism was attained. The psychology of his childhood and adolescent formation are important too, but obviously a line must be drawn somewhere— we will simply have to assume that during those formative years he reacted as any normal boy would to *his own special circumstances.* They were very special circumstances and again, despite all the New Critics may say, they must be regarded as a very direct cause of his successive points of view and of his choice of manner of reaction. With these preliminary but necessary warnings out of the way, let us look at his special circumstances as they affected his life and work within the framework of the background outlined in the first five chapters.

I *Biographical Data*

Carlos Fuentes was born in Mexico City on November 11, 1928. It is an index of his character that even this trivial but inevitable datum is not easily available. Emmanuel Carballos, a close associate in the 1950's, in his *Cuentistas mexicanos modernos (Modern Mexican Short Story Writers),* Mexico, 1956, gives the year of Fuentes' birth as 1929. In his subsequent *Diecinueve protagonistas de la literatura mexicana del siglo XX (Nineteen Representative Figures of Twentieth Century Mexican Literature),* Mexico, 1965, Carballos corrects the error. This bit of minutia is of interest only because Fuentes himself has taken a puckish delight in obscuring this and many other details of his life.[1]

Fuentes' upbringing and education reflect the peripatetic quality of the family life during his childhood and early youth. Since his father was a career diplomat, it was inevitable that the boy would be exposed to the varying influences attendant on the itinerant character of a diplomat's life of transfers from post to post. His primary and secondary schooling were achieved in Washington, D. C., Santiago (Chile), Buenos Aires, and Mexico City. Later, when his father's posts included European as well as American capitals, he also studied in Geneva. His early introduction to the culture of the United States gave him the advantage of learning English at the age of four, so that he is truly bilingual.

French was not learned until much later (1950), when he had some idea of studying international law and of becoming a diplomat himself. His university education was begun at Catholic University in Washington and completed at the National University of Mexico (School of Law).

All this may explain why Fuentes himself should have a taste for the peripatetic life, and it gives an indication of the many influences that went into forming his personality. If being a Mexican just by itself implies a hybrid development, even in one who never leaves his country and does all his schooling at home, how much more so must this quality be evident in a man like Fuentes who, from a very early age, was forced by childhood circumstances to defend himself as a Mexican and to inquire in his own mind what it meant to be a Mexican. Children in Washington are no more polite than they are anywhere else and Fuentes was often driven to angry assertions of his own national integrity not only by the childish attacks of little playmates but by the generally provincial attitude of many North Americans towards other nationalities. Especially in the movies of those times, he found much to be angry about as Mexicans were generally "bad" men and little attempt was made to present historical truth in regard to the War with Mexico or about the many interventions the United States has permitted itself in the lands of its neighbor.[2] So chauvinism on the part of the "gringos" was met with chauvinism on the part of young Carlos. Yet, being, an intelligent boy, he knew that one has to meet attacks not only on their own level but also on a higher, more rational level as well.

II *Implications of His Early Formation*

He was thus inevitably led, nay, forced, as were all intelligent, well-educated men of Mexico of his generation, to make an inquiry into his own history and to seek for a definition first of Mexico itself and then of himself as a Mexican. No man of intelligence is satisfied with chauvinism and it would be just as limiting to become a "professional Mexican" as it must be to be a "super-American"—and more difficult, since the economic and military inferiority of Mexico vis-à-vis its more powerful neighbor has to be carefully distinguished from other differences which are not so quantitatively "inferiorities." Whereas the North American can often fall into a careless acceptance of the notion that economic and military superiority also mean social and ideological superiority, the Mexican, faced by his own history, cannot so easily deceive himself. So Carlos Fuentes, like all men of his generation in Mexico, was obliged to study his own history, especially that of the Revolution and its aftermath, and to make his own appraisal of what it all meant.

The itinerant diplomatic life was thus not only an advantage because of the contact it provided with other languages and cultures, but also because of the psychological perception it gave of one's own language and culture as seen from a different point of view. Some of Fuentes' ideas on language and style are definitely traceable to his early contact with English (and will be discussed more fully in Chapter 10); while his preoccupation with Mexico, its history, and the quality of Mexicanism, are a theme of some of his novels. In other words, his own personal interpretation of history and his own quality as a Mexican provide the background, framework, and point of view of his major works. His personal knowledge of history would at first be like that of most children, emotional. Such a simple patriotic reaction was modified over the years by much reading in many sources so that eventually it became a cultural understanding of the facts and movements of national history itself. Only later would it be modified even further by a psychological comprehension of the meaning of history, also achieved by reading, contacts, and actual living amongst other men of similar formation.[3] So a recital of where his schooling was obtained is of value only as an indication of where this diverse exposure led.

Family life is a developmental factor that is very risky to assess. Schooling can be assessed easily in comparison. Because again inevitably, a child starts off by accepting uncritically all that his family is and stands for—its attitudes are his. Only later, as he matures and widens his own experience, does he begin to wonder about these attitudes, begin to question them, begin to rebel against them as insufficient, even, perhaps, as unacceptable. The whole process of psychological maturation in a youth is the subject of endless discussions by professionally trained psychologists; all we can say here is that the intensity of the inevitable rebellion is in proportion to the emotional nature of the individual. It may be acute or relatively mild. Fuentes, as a writer, has the escape valve of projection of his own emotional conflicts into his work, and he himself says that the autobiographical elements in *The Good Conscience* (discussed more fully in Chapter 8) are due to the fact that his writing of this work coincided with (interesting that he does not say it was inspired by) a moment of rupture, "very traumatic," with his own family, with his own past, his own middle-class upbringing in all its aspects.[4]

III *Rupture with the Past*

This was in 1954, and the rupture alluded to included his decision to "live his own life" as a writer and no longer to work towards or plan to be an international diplomat or lawyer. This was a major decision since a great deal of work and preparation had already gone into the original, family plan. He had studied international law in Geneva, he had been a member of the Mexican delegation to the International Labor Organization, he had been a cultural attaché to the Embassy in Geneva, he had held bureaucratic posts in the University of Mexico, he had been head of the Ministry of Foreign Affairs' Department of Cultural Relations. Not only was this career a "natural" one for him, made easier for him by his father's established connections in this field, but his family's bourgeois tradition and history (his paternal grandfather, for example, had been a banker) indicated a professional career of respectability and dignity, and furthermore his own personality and presence, charming and attractive, seemed to guarantee success. Why not accept, as Jaime Ceballos, the protagonist of *The Good Conscience* does, all that his family could provide and all that it stood for? Why turn his back on all that and join the amusing but rather disreputable world of "Bohemia"—writers, theatrical people, talented riffraff with no standards and no position? It was indeed a rupture. Worse yet, not only did he turn his back on respectability and social reputation (although artists were beginning to be seen, even in "good" society), but he went further, he became politically a traitor to his class as well, he became a Marxist. Such a decision was as sensational and as tragic as would be the declaration by a young

Spanish aristocrat in the court of Philip II that he had become a
Lutheran![5]

IV *First Independent Efforts*

But what had been an avocation now became his vocation. He
had always written as a teenager and as a young man; and
even as a child his imagination had pointed toward some sort of
future expression in the literary arts. His mother had, naturally,
been proud of her talented son (there is only one other child, his
sister Elisa), and his father certainly would not have objected to
the burgeoning young diplomat's being a "gentleman-writer" in
his spare time. But Carlos found himself unable to accept the
comfortable solution, and his personal rebellion was made the
more indignant and angry by his acceptance of the Marxian
theories of value and of history. Marxism seemed to offer him an
acceptable rationalization for his emotional reaction to the social
injustices that made him intolerant of the world he inhabited.
His interests became increasingly literary and political. He was
a cofounder (with Emmanuel Carballos, previously mentioned)
of the *Revista Mexicana de Literatura (Mexican Review of Literature)*, which subscribed to the theory that a culture can be profitably national only when it is generously universal; he wrote for
leftist magazines *(Siempre! [Always!], Política [Politics])*, and
published (in 1954) his first collection of short stories, *Los días
enmascarados (The Masked Days)*.

The attraction of Marxism or, in its everyday application to
world problems, Communism, seems, for the young, to be based
on an emotional appeal. At least it was in the case of Fuentes.
Like most young men, he was idealistic about helping the down-
trodden of the earth to lose their chains, about storming the man-
sions of the oppressors (amongst whom, somehow, the shocked
faces of one's parents and other hateful authorities are dimly
seen), about seeing oneself in the "vanguard of the proletariat,"
leading a singing, victorious multitude to social justice in spite of
the cynical oligarchy that has exploited everyone so long. It is
necessary for us to try to understand this appeal of Marxism for
the young: the appeal is chiefly to their ardor and anger, to feed-
ing the indignation they feel on discovering as true what they

only suspected, that the world is run by wicked, greedy men, by bribes and corruption. Then they read their own history, and, in the case of Mexicans, they find that a scant fifty years before the whole country was ablaze in an effort to remedy this shameful condition. Then they look around them and discover that somehow the Revolution was "betrayed" and their world is again in the hands of the oligarchy, tired, greedy, and cynical. Then some more enlightened schoolmate shows them that the Revolution was really bourgeois (in spite of its peasant heroes), and that the *real* Revolution is yet to be won. If you are a young man like Carlos Fuentes, who has charm and a facile pen, you will be cultivated by the devious little "leaders" with the foreign accents since you can provide many articles that will influence other young men and persuade them to support the camouflaged causes which may eventually bring about a change in the power structure. All this was operative on Fuentes, as it has been on many another young idealist, and it still goes on: only last year a well-known columnist of the magazine *Siempre!* was arrested, among others, as one of the leaders of a small group of revolutionaries who had a good-sized cache of arms and bombs with which to overthrow the government.[6]

Despite his usefulness, however, Fuentes either never penetrated to or was never accepted by that inner circle of Marxist leaders who are notoriously leery of the intellectuals because they are not reliable. It is interesting that intellectuals should thus be classified by the self-constituted real "vanguard of the proletariat" since it is one of the chief causes for the defection, later, of intellectuals from the Party. Hell hath no fury like an intellectual scorned. Very possibly this "unreliability" of intellectuals as such is quite justifiably guarded against, since they are quite capable of convincing themselves of any intellectual position that happens to suit their own inner needs of the moment, and are equally capable of turning against the Party in the name of academic liberty, or artistic freedom of expression, or even of intellectual integrity, whenever their intellectual vanity has been wounded by a deviationist or bourgeois label. Diego Rivera, expelled from the Party for the second time, was called a "Trotskyite Zapatista agrarian of the petty bourgeoisie," and Rivera was not even a real intellectual. Fuentes, who had been writing "theoretical" articles on ideological issues (in a journalistic manner) for *Política* (well known for its slavish following of the Party line), broke with the Party (along with several other intellectuals) in 1962, in the name of intellectual integrity. In that same year, 1962, he had been denied a visa to enter the United States, the State Department cautiously stating that he was "possibly a Communist." His purpose in applying for a visa was to accept an invitation by NBC to debate an assistant secretary on U.S. policy in Latin America.[7] One might say that the State Department was wise to avoid the debate on any pretext since U.S. history in Latin America is one of the most vulnerable points in the armor of "fortress America."

But there is an interesting and delicate relationship between Fuentes' break with *Política* and the Party and his retreat into the ranks of "acceptable" avant-garde intellectuals who no longer noisily insist on the overthrow of the U.S. imperialist octopus as a *sine qua non* to the solution of the world's problems. The State Department has since become sophisticated enough and relaxed enough to recognize that a "Marxist" is not necessarily a revolutionary in the bomb-throwing sense of the word, and many revolutionaries have seen the wisdom of joining the ranks of the more acceptable "Marxists" in order to subsist in a world that is still—a great deal of it—living under the sway of the octopus.

What is being suggested here cannot be developed any further since it is impossible to penetrate completely into the motivations that impel any man. Nor is there any sly condemnation implied of an intellectual for using whatever weapons or means he has for dealing with the world as it is and making his way in it. However, it is vitally important for the understanding of any writer, and this writer in particular, to consider as objectively as possible all the factors that have influenced him to choose the particular course he has chosen. We all make compromises and psychological "accommodations"; to do so is one of the indications of the transition between impulsive, heedless youth and more mature consideration of what is best for us. And no writer could have written *The Good Conscience* or penetrated so accurately into the psychology of Jaime Ceballos who had not himself walked the same path and suffered the same crises (the same in mode, but not necessarily in manner). There are, as

Ortega y Gasset points out, many possibilities in the circumstances offered by our lovely new world, and they become lovelier if one will simply make an easy "accommodation"—there is great leeway now in the type of "capitulation" one may make (perhaps it may not even be recognized as a capitulation), and the rewards are great; ability to live one's own life, to develop one's own talents, to cultivate one's own garden (literally and figuratively), to have "a large, rambling house . . . in a shady residential suburb . . .," a beautiful and well-known actress for a wife, much material comfort, participation in the international set life—all the delights provided by the imperialist octopus society for those who will "fall in line" acceptably.[8] To recognize one's own failure, one's own weakness, as Jaime Ceballos does, can also be "an act of honesty" (as Fuentes himself says about the protagonist of this book). And thus intellectual integrity is preserved and one gets what one wants.

V *Towards Maturity*

Aside from the developmental importance of all this in Fuentes' own work, there is a further corollary to be deduced (and which is stated in Chapter 9)—it is unwise to take an intellectual as one's guide to the modern labyrinth. Until he developed his own intellectual maturity, Fuentes went down many paths pointed out to him by his contemporary intellectual peers. Just to consider a partial list of the analysts of the Revolution and its aesthetic implications, all of whom have influenced Fuentes and his generation in their successive points of view, will give us an idea of the range of perspectives that can be adopted, one after the other, or at times concurrently, by a conscientious intellectual. One whole set of novelists (the older generation: Azuela, Guzmán, Vasconcelos) regards the Revolution with varying degrees of pessimism; the poets either stand aloof (Amado Nervo, Luis Urbina) or say that it has been "insufficient" (Octavio Paz); the great painters of "the Mexican school" (Diego Rivera, Orozco, Siqueiros) have erratically pointed toward Communism as its ultimate fulfillment; the calm intellectuals (like Alfonso Reyes) have sought aesthetic solutions or chosen the Ivory Tower. In short, each man must, after as full a consideration as possible of all the implications, after considering all the claims put forward by his intellectual peers, and compatibly to his own temperament,—each man must make up his own mind, choose his own path, decide on his own "accommodation" with things as they are, and then proceed from there. This is what Fuentes did in the late 1950's and early 1960's and as a consequence, it is interesting to observe, since 1962 his polemical articles are fewer and his literary articles more frequent.

As Fuentes has matured, oddly enough, he has become less able to accept Mexico as a permanent residence. Whether this constitutes a further rejection of so-called roots or whether it is a confirmation of the wandering pattern established during his childhood does not matter—the important thing is that he is becoming more of a cosmopolitan and is no longer primarily considering, or concerned with, what it means to be Mexican. This is particularly evident in his second (1964) book of short stories, *Cantar de ciegos (Songs of the Blind),* all of which are much more cosmopolitan in theme even where the protagonist or setting is Mexican. Also it must be considered that the life of a gregarious writer in Mexico City is fairly restricted and it is not always easy to escape the "phonies" who also inhabit the bohemian cafe-society world. In Europe it is easy, when one is tired of Paris, to run off to Rome or London or Barcelona; in Mexico, where is there to run off to? Acapulco is even worse than Mexico City. Also, say what you will, Paris, London, Rome—Europe, in short—for all their "decadence" and tiredness, also still provide more intellectual stimulation than New York, with its omnipresent commercialism, and immeasurably more than Mexico City which, in spite of its size, is still remote and provincial compared to the European capitals.

There are other reasons too for Fuentes' decision to leave Mexico. Many of them are personal and psychologically important but need not be commented on here. After all, he is over forty—an age at which a man is again forced to examine himself, what he is, what he has done, what he is doing, what he wants to do with the time remaining. One can no longer play the role of the angry young novelist. The youth has disappeared, the anger has either mellowed or turned sour, the early solutions are no longer so attractive; a second rebellion, against age, sets in.

All these factors enter into his decision. Also, one must consider the fact that the literary world, in Mexico as elsewhere, is a tendentious world of petty intrigues, gossip, and neurotic interest in the personal life of one's neighbor. Fuentes is not yet ready to buy a villa in Cuernavaca and settle down to being the grand old man of Mexican letters.

What has happened, it would seem, is that Fuentes has moved with the world and it is no longer so obsessively important to him to define Mexico or Mexicanism, or even to fight for a solution to the woes of the masses. He is more interested now in the relationship of man with his fellow man (and woman) and their situation in time. Other questions interest him—the working out of individual destinies affected by the collective subconscious, the myth, the correlation between reality and fantasy (and what these are), the merging and separation of personality with itself and with that of others, psychic alienation—all themes that transcend nationality and economics and have to do with the human condition in almost a metaphysical sense. All this, it might be said, is simply a part of the process of maturing. Indeed it is, but the way and the direction one takes in maturing is also a result of what one has been and what one has been formed by, and we cannot understand the new Fuentes without first understanding the previous Fuentes who was formed by the background outlined in the previous chapters. He is a complicated man and his complications can be only partially penetrated at best.

For deeper penetration into what it means to be a writer, the interested reader can find many insights in the findings of psychologists who have specialized in studying writers. One plausible theory is that of Dr. Edmund Bergler, previously mentioned, who offers (and, of course, substantiates his hypothesis with a wealth of peritinent evidence) the idea that the creative writer is essentially a neurotic personality, a compulsive neurotic who must write in order to sublimate successfully a severe inner conflict that will not give him peace in any other way. According to Bergler, this sublimation is accompanied by a painful and depressing struggle within the artist which can only be endured because creative writing is an inner necessity. Bergler states categorically (in *The Writer and Psychoanalysis*) that all writers (and he extends this deduction to all types of artistic creativity) are unconsciously chronic defendants on trial before their own inner tribunal, and that their work reflects, in a disguised fashion, the inner alibis they present to their own accusatory inner conscience. How the creative artist develops this neurosis in the first place is described. Bergler makes a very good case for his conclusions with analyses of Stendhal, Proust, and other writers.[9] No matter what one's reaction may be to the neo-Freudian description of personality, these ideas must certainly be taken into account in considering any writer, especially one as complicated as Carlos Fuentes. Whether he is actually a compulsive neurotic or not can be left to the psychiatrists to determine—there is no question that he does (who does not?) show in his life some symptoms that could be labelled neurotic and that these symptoms are in turn reflected in his writings. He himself says he is a "talking machine." People who talk excessively, who suffer from logorrhea, as the psychoanalytic jargon has it, do so because they wish to stifle or shut up, not the person with whom they are ostensibly conversing, but the inner voice that constantly accuses them. Of what? That is their secret. In substantiation of all this, consider Fuentes' own statement that he is "a hypochondriac at work . . . [that he writes] with the nerves of my stomach, and pay for it with a duodenal ulcer and a chronic colic."[10]

So, not only are we dealing with an unreliable intellectual, but also with a compulsive neurotic. We bother because it is from such men that insights come, that our own experience is enriched, that poetry is made. In the following chapters it will be shown, it is hoped, that Carlos Fuentes is an important writer with a great deal to say, not only because he suffers from logorrhea, but because what he says is worth saying and worth listening to.

CHAPTER 7

The Short Stories

TO trace the course of human development since the Renaissance is to catalogue the steps which have led us in our day to the dehumanitazion of man. John Updike summarizes it most succinctly:

First went supernatural faith, then faith in kings, then faith in reason, then faith in nature, then faith in science, and, most lately, faith in the subconscious.

The next step is the loss of faith in human nature and this perhaps final step is, it seems, already epidemic in our society. The course of development in the arts has been parallel; as Updike says, "The texture of prose and the art of narration have changed to fit the case"; and, in passing, he points out that "indeed, since *Don Quixote* fiction has to some extent thrived on disillusion." But the process has gone far beyond disillusion, of course, and

. . .in this century the minimal presupposition of human significance . . . seems too much to be assumed. [All this] renders obsolete the interconnectedness of action that comprises "plot" and the trust in communication that gives a narration voice and pulse. Formless tales blankly told may be the end result . . .[1]

We have not only reached the point he indicates but are already passing it. Much of contemporary literature is already pointing out the void and many of the "characters" in this "literature" are already more humanoid than human.[2] Formless tales blankly told are already the norm in certain little magazines. This is the

logical end of the extreme materialist position, the inevitable conclusion of the behaviorist assertion that human nature is after all
nothing but a series of mechanical conditioned reflexes. The
squirming caused in the artist as he tries despairingly to reconcile this logic to his own desire for self-expression is what produces much of our current tortured prose.

Carlos Fuentes, resting on the Objectivist ledge, taking refuge
in his version of the *nouveau roman,* has only recently reached
the perilous point he is at in his current development. When he
first started writing seriously in the 1950's, he had not yet fore-
seen the logical end of his beginning, and his first productions
were frankly experimental. However, even then, the selectivity
which must operate in any artist had already inclined him toward a certain type of experiment rather than another. The literature he was exposed to and his own choice of reading influenced
his own first efforts and we can easily see traces of Poe, Rimbaud,
and Horacio Quiroga in his early short stories which have been
characterized as "clearly a tour-de-force by a young writer."[3]

I Los días enmascarados ("The Masked Days")

His first collection was published in 1954 with the title *Los
días enmascarados* ("The Masked Days"), not yet translated
into English. It presents six short stories "fantastic in theme and
ironic in style."[4] The fantasy of the themes shifts from the macabre to the heavily playful, and the irony of the style from the
subtle to the labored. A young writer, at the beginning of his
career, rarely has a developed style and tends to fluctuate between a simple, direct narrative and too much involution. We
can see this clearly in these six tales.

The titles of the six stories are: 1. "Chac Mool," 2. "En defensa
de la Trigolibia" ("In Defense of Trigolibia"), 3. "Tlactocatzine,
del jardín de Flandes" ("Tlactocatzine, the One from the Flem-
ish Garden"), 4. "Letanía de la orquídea" ("Litany of the Orchid"). 5. "Por boca de los Dioses" ("The Gods Speak"), and 6.
"El que inventó la pólvora" ("The Man Who Invented Gun-
powder"). The first and fifth are tales that show young Fuentes'
horrified fascination with the primitive deities of his country.
The second and sixth express his interest in manipulating lan-

guage and his rejection of capitalist technology. The third is a forerunner of his novelette, *Aura*—concerned with age and myth. The fourth, in Freudian terms, is an anal-erotic fantasy on the medieval punishment for sodomy—impalement. A Freudian exegesis could be applied to all these stories, since they are all preoccupied with what is evidently young Fuentes' reaction to theories of the unconscious and its expression by Surrealism. The unconscious, in fact, is the theme that connects them all. In Fuentes' view, as expressed here, the primitive deities of Mexico are forms of projection of the unconscious, symbolizing horrible instincts of the human heart, mostly cannibalistic and self-devouring. Filiberto in "Chac Mool," Oliverio in "Por boca de los Dioses," are both quite mad and wander in panic through a distorted world that is the fantasied embodiment of their own fears. Oliverio is the more developed of the two characters, he participates more in the self-devouring process, he kills a little old bore who has annoyed him (cf. the "old man" in Poe's story, "The Tell-tale Heart"); he steals a pair of lips off a painting, which in turn pursue him and run from him like dreadful incarnate blobs of living flesh; he visits the underworld, in the bowels of his hotel, into which he is plunged by a reluctant elevator, and where he is almost torn to pieces by the howling pantheon of Mexico that now resides there. Finally he is destroyed in the erotic embrace of the incarnate female deity, Tlazol, just as Filiberto is pursued and destroyed, even to Acapulco, by the animate statue of the Chac Mool. The stories are told with flashes of irony and macabre humor, by juxtaposing idiocies of modern life with idiocies of primitive life. Both stories are a child's nightmare dressed in the Surrealist trappings of a modern Red Riding Hood. The Wolf is the horrible deities that still reign in the human heart and lay in wait for us in the jungle-like woods of the human soul. Grandmother is the myth which suddenly throws off its disguise, its mask, to reveal the gleaming fangs, the writhing lips that lure, that pursue, that devour. The child wakes screaming, but it is a sophisticated child who sees the night-light and accepts the comfort of outward reality although it is not too sure in its heart that the old inner fear, evoked, monster-like, in its dream may not be the real reality, lurking just outside the door, waiting to pounce as soon as the eyes are closed.

These stories are forceful, effective, and semiconvincing. They convince us when the mood of horror is sustained and then simultaneously destroy the conviction when some idiotic irrelevancy is imposed on the horror. Is this technique—a conscious attempt to portray the unconscious—or is it the talent of a young writer, still not entirely sure of what he can do? Perhaps a combination of both: the technique not yet fully mastered; the talent, not yet sure of the direction it is to take. In any case, these stories are interesting because of the new setting for old themes (the city of Mexico) and new vestments of old themes (the primitive gods of Mexico). Also, let us admit it, Fuentes has the sovereign ability that all writers must have—he is able to tell a tale, to "spin a yarn," to weave the spell—an ability without which no writer can succeed. It is not simply technique, although much of it is (apt metaphors, smooth transitions, psychologically acceptable associations). It is that quality that seems to be innate in good writers and that is the despair of critics because it is almost impossible to define. Artistic perception, intuitive awareness—call it what you will—it is undoubtedly an innate quality, what makes a man a writer rather than a tailor. Part of it is a preoccupation with words, which is well expressed in the playful second story.

In "En defensa de la Trigolibia" the author, drunk with the power to manipulate words, displays a virtuosity that can be compared to that of a young violinist showing off with one of Paganini's more difficult caprices. The setting, what the story is about, the excuse for this coruscation, is a tiny satire in the "plague on both your houses" vein; the Nusitanios, who represent the United States, after proclaiming a Declaration of the Trigolibios of Man, in which the inalienable right of all men to free trigolibing is set forth, find themselves at odds in their interpretation and application of these inalienable rights with Tundriusa, representing the U.S.S.R. The latter points out dialectically that true trigolibing can exist only under certain conditions which, naturally, are to be found only in Tundriusa. The dialectical form lends itself admirably to this sophomoric exercise in satire, which any smart undergraduate could dash off for the school paper in half an hour. It is hardly worthwhile to mention the George Orwell influence. It is more interesting to observe that Fuentes seems to be expressing disillusion with Russia. That he is also expressing disillusion with the United States is simply a form of conventionality—it is practically obligatory in certain intellectual circles abroad to talk of the United States, if at all, with jesting disdain. But that, in the early 1950's, a young writer should publicly poke fun at the Soviet Union was not so conventional. Historically, it is interesting to observe the attitudes taken in turn by the young intellectuals who metamorphose from angry young men to disillusioned young men to cynical young men. In the process of growing up, they occasionally leave interesting artifacts behind them. And that is just about what ". . . Trigolibia" is.

"El que inventó la pólvora" is also a satire, somewhat less sophomoric this time, on technological obsolescence. The usefulness of a spoon, for example, is reduced from an indefinite period to a week, then to seventy-two hours, at which time it turns into gelatin. Very soon the revolt of the "things" extends to toothbrushes, writing desks, shoes, and soon becomes universal—all manufactured articles turn into heaps of trash until finally this "new Industrial Revolution," or technological malady, attacks man and nothing is left but the narrator, who starts over by rubbing two sticks together. A slight effort, perhaps a little better than " . . . Trigolibia," since it is is Huxley rather than Orwell from whom it derives.

"Letanía de la orquídea" is told with more control and with more artistic pretension; the language is more selective and the figures of speech more apt. However, it too is a finger exercise. In all these tales (excepting possibly the third), Fuentes is "performing," practicing at the keyboard, amusing himself by producing variations on themes. This is a perfectly legitimate pastime for a young artist and may even provide half-an-hour's entertainment for the idle reader. But we need not take these études too seriously—they are slight and are of interest chiefly for the indications they give of Fuentes' interests, attitudes, external preoccupations, and trends. As we shall see in his second volume of short stories, some of his themes are repeated, developed, and more expertly handled.

In this fourth story, a small ironic study of inversion, we see again, a little more subtly arranged, the juxtaposition of incongruities, and adherence to realism of presentation (enhancing the fantasy of content), the deliberate selection of detail to emphasize the point of view. Here there seems to be more mastery of technique than in " . . . Trigolibia"—the writer is surer of himself, virtuosity is no longer necessary. There are even experiments with stylistic syncopation that foreshadow the influence of Dos Passos in the first novel. Again, the story itself is almost beside the point. In Panama (the humidity, rain, heat: the tropical atmosphere), Muriel, a young female impersonator (the exotic, the unusual), finds a luxuriant orchid sprouting from his coccyx. Cutting a hole in his trousers so that this gorgeous flower may freely wave, he goes to his mulatto dance hall and is a great success (the outlandish, the hilariously pathetic). Back in his room at the end of the evening, he cuts off the flower at the root, planning to sell it (the double switch: perversion of a perversion), but from the stump now grows a splintery stake that turns inward and impales him/her. The "realism" of the next-to-last paragraph is calculated to make the reader gasp. It may be dismissed as an example of the fallacy of intention, as well as further evidence of the writer's youthfulness—what reader gasps anymore, what writer tries to make him do so?

We have left until last the best story of the collection, "Tlactocatzine, del jardín de Flandes." This is a subtle evocation of a mood, the mood of nostalgia, in a setting of vaguely eerie circumstances. There are metaphysical changes of time and even of place, as though H. G. Wells had decided to write a story in the style of Henry James. The mood is Jamesian, perhaps, but the style is still too Wellsian, too abrupt, too chronological. Two well-known critics have pointed out that " . . . the pattern of poetry resides primarily in its arrangement of language, and the pattern of prose fiction primarily in its arrangement of action." Action, of course, is simply "a progression from one position or one point of awareness to another."[5] But the progression need not be chronological; as a matter of fact, loss of subtlety is precisely the result of such a straightforward progression. In a short story of only ten pages, however, there is no room for too much subtlety and the writer must, as indirectly but as economically as possible, proceed to create his effect. This is done by a description, artfully presented, of the old house, built during the period of the French Intervention, with its faded elegances, its great salon, its tapestried library—all this is transferred to the

young narrator, who falls under the spell of the house—and the
ambience is prepared for the apparition. First, the garden, which
opens only off the library, is not a Mexican garden, the tones are
too muted, there is no sun. The young man ventures into the
garden and meets the faded apparition of a mad old lady, and
the odor of death and the unearthly rain are all about. In the end
he cannot escape from the garden and he is a prisoner forever of
the mad ghost who is Carlota, Empress of Mexico.

This story is, on the whole, well done; the transitions, the deepening of the mood, are handled skillfully, the language changes,
as we penetrate more deeply into the action, from colloquial to
poetic, and, finally, we are moved by the capturing of the pathos
of age and madness. The fact that the ghost in the story is none
other than Carlota is partially an indication of a romantic interest on the part of the author. This whole episode of the French
Intervention in Mexico has been of great romantic interest to
several Mexican writers, and one may almost gauge their real
social attitude toward being Mexican by their treatment of the
Carlota legend, acceptance of the pathos from a romantic sentimentality, or rejection of the whole legend from an almost historical indignation. Actually, we need not read too much into the
author's intention here, since it has little actual bearing on his
performance (except, of course, to inspire it), but it is a point to
bear in mind, since it ties in with some of the information in the
previous chapter and must be amplified slightly in the last chapter. Of more importance is the fact that this story is a rehearsal,
we might say, for the novelette, *Aura,* which is considered in the
next chapter. Let us keep in mind therefore the performance here
to see how the fuller orchestration is handled later.

Parenthetically, we should say that in case any reader is feeling querulous about the critical judgments made on these stories
of the first collection, he might prefer to read over the first few
pages of the last chapter, in which we state, as far as is possible
or necessary for an essay of this type, what critical norms have
been used as guidelines for evaluation of the whole corpus of
Fuentes' work.

To sum up on this first collection. In "Chac Mool" and "Por
boca de los Dioses," the author's preoccupation is with the im-

pact—the *residual* impact—of the primitive gods on the subconscious mind (his own, primarily) of a man who was born of Mexican heritage and who must, therefore, come to terms with that heritage. The presentation in both cases is ironic, fantastical, Surrealistic. It is as though a young, modern writer feels somehow obliged to deal with this aspect of his heritage but resents having to do so and therefore mocks it. There may indeed be some artistic acceptance of the Jungian theory of the collective unconscious, a theory which, as we all know, has had much influence on writers ever since it was proposed. These primitive gods, being monstrous and annihilative, must be rejected, after having been used as part of a Surrealistic setting. The fact that they kill the two protagonists in the stories is part of the rejection, since these protagonists, in their weak-mindedness, are also aspects of the personality which must be destroyed. Part of this feeling seems to come briefly into play in "Tlactocatzine. . . .," since Carlota calls Maximilian by the name the Mexicans gave him, in their language, and furthermore the last four words of her closing monologue (or ravings) are in the language of the Aztec. This presumably was meant to show that somehow the Aztec gods were responsible for Carlota's madness or posssession. This is entirely fantastical on the part of the author, since there is no evidence that her madness had any "Aztec" overtones at all. There are innumerable facets to the author's preoccupation with these aspects of the subconscious and its partial intrusion into the third story. Unfortunately we cannot take the space here to investigate them further, although they are well worth thinking about in themselves, in connection with contemporary Mexican literature as a whole and Fuentes' work in particular.

Perhaps we have dealt a little harshly with ". . . Trigolibia" and ". . . pólvora." They are of contributory importance since it is precisely through work of this sort, of little value in itself, that a young writer develops his talent and explores attitudes. Young writers who are exploring the world as well as attitudes also occasionally feel the need to deal with themes that in themselves have no particular attraction for them—in a way, this too is a developmental exercise since all themes, all human passions, are grist in the writer's mill. This may account for the tale about the orchidaceous Muriel, although it is worth-while noting that the

same theme, in a much more straightforward fashion, is again
dealt with in the second collection, which we shall consider
shortly.

And there we have the first public bow—a slight collection and
one which did not stir up either much fuss or much interest when
it was first published. The date of the publication of a collection has little to do with the importance of the stories in it for the
development of the writer, since in most cases the stories were
written long before publication date, probably reworked and re-
written before finally being collected, and published only when
the author's reputation is wide enough to warrant the hope that
there may be some profit in offering such a collection to the public at that time. We must not forget, in our concern for literary
values, that publishing is a business and commercial values often
override aesthetic ones. Chronologically, Fuentes' next work is
his first novel, *Where the Air Is Clear*, but from a point of view
of genre, it is more to our purpose to continue here with a consideration of the short stories and to take up next, therefore, the
second collection.

II   Cantar de ciegos ("Songs of the Blind")

First published in 1964, *Cantar de ciegos* ("Songs of the Blind")
is an assortment of seven tales, all far superior in depth of penetration and in technique to the first group we have just considered. In the ten years between the two collections, the development of the writer as an artist is formidable and exciting.
Of course, by 1964 he had already produced two novels, both of
which, being experimental in direction, served to further
his development enormously. The stories have been produced
concomitantly and not always originally as stories since during
this period Fuentes was interested in and working actively with
the cinematographic circles in the Mexican capital. In a relatively small artistic milieu, such as is inevitable in a compact country like England or in a centralized country like Mexico
(or like France, for that matter), there is a great deal of com-
mingling of arts and artists, everyone knows everyone else, everyone knows what so-and-so is up to, not only professionally but in
his private life as well, and Bohemia meets regularly in the same

places and for the same occasions, so it is the most natural thing in the world for a director or an actress to suggest casually to a promising writer that he might find it interesting to try his hand at a scenario or a script. Quite often it turns out that a novelist is unable to adjust to the demands of the theatre (and the movies are a form of theatre) in that he is unable to work with a team since he is used to solitary creativity. Or, for aesthetic or social reasons, he finds the movies crass, vulgar, unsatisfactory. Fuentes himself has always insisted that "the rebuilding of the movies in Mexico is not a technical problem but one that is essentially human and social."[6] He feels that the themes of an authentic cinematographic art in Mexico should be drawn from the collective life of Mexicans, of their present-day collective life, a life which he feels is infinitely diversified. In other words, he recognizes that Mexico, within its own framework, has joined the great world in direction and interest. And he feels that the youth of Mexico (of which he is, of course, a part) is carrying to completion that psychological revolution which its grandparents started, but in a manner much more honest and much more direct than that of the older generation.

So, in spite of the fact that Fuentes himself disclaims in these stories any intent at "writing for the cinema,"[7] it is most likely that there was a close connection between the actual scriptwork he was doing at the time and the conception of some of these tales. Compartmentalization would be strange in anyone with such a zest for living totally as Fuentes has shown—it is no more possible for him to separate the creative segments of his personality than it would be for him to subdivide his personal life. Whatever else he may be, he is not a schizophrenic. And yet the whole question of his creative life is infinitely complicated by the fact that he is also an intellectual. So much so that occasionally it gets in his way, in the sense that the intellectual of his sort is more prone than other men to rationalization. This makes him untrustworthy as a sociologist or as an explainer of his own motivations, although it may make him a very good novelist. This intellectual subtlety in reasoning (in Fuentes it seems to be almost an Italian trait), deviousness perhaps, may be expressed in apparently quite straightforward language in conversation or in interviews, giving the impression of a sincere man groping honestly toward reasonable answers. Such an impression can be most deceptive and it will be discussed further, in Chapter 10. We must not allow it to lead us astray.

The attitude common to these stories is that modern society is decadent, rotten, and that the few "decent" individuals encountered are destroyed by it. Fuentes has not yet become an Objectivist, so he does not simply present this corruption but implies a moral position, an implicit condemnation. It is loss of innocence that is the common theme on the psychological level in these stories. But what kind of innocence can be lost in this modern world where nothing is innocent anymore, and who can be the loser? That is the subtlety that has been noted. Despite the general decadence and rottenness surrounding us in all areas, there is still possible in some areas an innocence which may be, actually, no more than naiveté or ignorance of the world, but which leads in any event, no matter what it is at bottom, to destruction of the innocent. This is almost the old metaphysical idea of sin, differently stated. But let us not get too subtle ourselves, or be beguiled by the intellectual's pastime of "reading into" a work of art possibly more than is actually there. Let us look at the works themselves for enlightenment.

It is difficult to say, on any meaningful level, which is the best of these stories. Usually in a collection of this sort, if the author has any interest in the matter at all, he will prefer to put the story he likes best at the beginning. Liking a certain story best does not mean that it *is* best, however; but in such a matter of taste, what test could be applied except that of the total effectiveness of the story—its impact, so to speak? But again, one man's impact may be another man's cushion. We can only state which of these stories seemed most effective, without then trying to rationalize this impression into a statement that tries to convince others. With stories of this calibre, so much superior to the first group, it is every man his own critic and no need to argue. So, let us take them in the order in which they are presented.

The first story, "Las dos Elenas" ("The Two Helens"), is a subtle study in scarlet, the scarlet of amorality. It is a triple character sketch built around a young wife, the first Helen, her husband Victor, and her mother, the second Helen. The wife, a very modern young woman, is trying to persuade her husband of the theoretical acceptability of the *menage-à-trois* as a way of life. Guy de Maupassant presented this idea long ago. What is new here is that the husband is already carrying on an affair with his mother-in-law, the second Helen. The tale depends for its full effectiveness on the "punch" ending à la O. Henry, when it is revealed that the man's mistress is in effect his wife's mother. The fact that the impact depends on this final revelation actually weakens the effect. Again, it is the implied moralistic attitude that the idea is somehow shocking which, in fact, destroys the shock. There is a remnant here of the old Marxist puritanism in the effect sought. The true decadent element is that the wife, the first Helen, is naively honest in *her* approach to the problem of marital boredom while her husband and her mother are playing the old game of adultery behind closed doors, in the old dishonest and traditional way. So the deepest level, it would seem, is the author's intent to show that modern so-called amorality may actually be the most innocent sort of naiveté when compared to the age-old dishonesty of the real serpent. Who is more immoral, Helen in her amorality, or Victor in his hidden adultery? And what about the mother? The fact that she is from the tropics —Veracruz—is brought out several times. Is this supposed to suggest a reason for *her* deception of her own husband and her daughter? If so, it is a deliberate cliché: women from the tropics are notoriously of easy virtue. Or is it simply "atmosphere"? There is no need for that sort of atmosphere in a story that takes place entirely in the highlands of Mexico City. It cannot be just an extraneous detail tossed in by the author. Selectivity here is high on his part and each detail contributes to the total effect. Perhaps it is an attempt to give a touch of morbidity to the story. This is more likely, since the tropical woman is still an effective stereotype of adulterous femininity.

Fuentes' style and method of presentation here is almost completely developed: the use of dialogue, the *art-nouveau* descriptions (like an Aubrey Beardsley illustration in prose), the incongruous realism (Helen matter-of-factly munches a sandwich as she discusses her visit to a brothel), the use of synesthesia—all elements of Fuentes' style, which he employs with great dexterity to contribute, independently and in combination, to produce the effect of naturalness. Again, one gets the impression of the sincere, straightforward, honest observer of life presenting a most subtle, devious tale that is effective and convincing. It is a *tour-de-force*, of course; but when a clever trick becomes habitual it is no longer simply a clever trick but becomes mastery. It is all very well to call the first collection by a young writer such a name, but that is no longer enough here. And this may be one of the reasons for the controversy around Fuentes—he is like a disarming child who runs up with an intricate artifice he has made and presents it for our attention. The first reaction is amazement and then suspicion—what is this seemingly straightforward man up to? And the first thing that becomes apparent is that he is not so straightforward as he seems. We have been taken in. Many readers (and critics) are annoyed by this, they feel it is insincere writing (see the last chapter for the reaction of Keith Botsford), but once we have caught on, there is no need to be annoyed, we can relax, admire the cleverness of the child, this *enfant terrible,* and enjoy the product he has contrived.

So subtle is the weaving of this story that there is even an alternate idea: all the way through the narrative Helen, the wife, uses the epithet *Nibelungo* as a pet name for her husband. He, Victor, who is the narrator, confesses he does not know why his wife calls him that. But we all know who the Nibelungs were, a race of demonic beings. Are we therefore supposed to infer that Helen knows that her husband's nature is demonic? Nothing would delight Fuentes more than to think that he has his reader so *enredado* (involved and confused), and what compounds the pleasure of this mischievous writer is that the more careful the reader the more *enredado* he will be. Just as Fuentes has developed a technique for the writing of these stories, so one must develop a technique for reading them. It is the same technique that must be used in regarding a contemporary painting or listening to a piece of modern music—one must not *seek* meanings, which are multiple and on many levels, rather one must simply be "open" to them, receptive. Perhaps in a way this is what the Objectivists originally had in mind when they spoke of "participation" and before they elaborated the thought into a dogma.

"La muñeca reina" ("The Doll Queen"), the second story, is an approach again to the *Aura* theme. The *Aura* theme, as in

"Tlactocatzine . . ." in the first collection, and as in the novelette *Aura* itself, is that of the reality of illusion, of hallucination. In "Tlactocatzine . . ." only one aspect of the idea is developed: the old enchantress who is really dead but who nevertheless draws the helpless young man into her spell, as her victim. In *Aura* this is further developed so that the aged enchantress has her complimentary aspect as a radiant young woman—this incarnation of the witch ensnares the hapless youth who, when he is about to possess his love finds he is embracing the old witch. In "La muñeca reina" the poetic and romantic young man, lost in the cold rain of the modern world, seeks again the innocent maiden who captivated him when he was an adolescent. He finds her but now she is a dreadful, vulgar invalid in a wheelchair, the captive of two sadistic parents who pretend that their beautiful little daughter Amilamia, whom the young man seeks, is dead. Thus they are free to victimize the monster that the real Amilamia has become. They have even gone so far as to keep their "dead" daughter's bedroom "as she left it," with a large doll dressed in her clothes on the bed, while the real Amilamia, paralyzed, cigarette smoking, hopelessly ordinary, is confined to her wheelchair in the back of the house. Again a variation on a theme: Coppelia, Pygmalion; but again with the "new twist," the modern touch—the combination of realism of presentation and fantastical horror of content, all skillfully evoked and displayed for our inspection, rather like a vampire bat found mounted among the gorgeous butterflies of a crazy lepidopterists's collection. The tale starts off with all the nostalgic loveliness of a child's fairy tale and suddenly it turns into a child's nightmare, and no longer a child's but an adult's. It is this element of horror that is hidden, hinted at, of the serpent behind the mask, that gives Fuentes' retelling of an old theme its immediacy. This sort of "switch" can be traced back to medieval ballads, and many writers have dressed old themes in new vestments. So let us not analyze this too thoroughly at the moment; it will be more appropriate in the discussion of *Aura,* in the next chapter.

The third story, "Fortuna lo que ha querido" ("What Fortune Brought"), presents a character sketch of an artist, a painter, and his preoccupation with sex which, although he does not realize it, seriously interferes with his ability to paint. Impressed by the single-minded dedication of great artists to their art, Fuentes seems to be telling himself (as much as us) that promiscuity inevitably dilutes art to say nothing of affecting the artist's vision of others: if they are objects of sexual satisfaction they are rarely also objects of art. "Fortuna . . ." is a slight story but is interesting because it illustrates in capsule form much of the style and attitude that Fuentes was to use in *Where the Air Is Clear*. The novel was published before the collection, but this particular story antedates the novel. Fuentes is not a prolific writer; his writing seems to require maximum utilization of all materials, which he reworks and reuses, and his inventiveness is more one of presentation than of themes. Even so, he seems always able to invest even reused material with a fresh appeal and interest so that one does not mind having met the idea before.

"Vieja Moralidad" ("The Old Morality"), the fourth story, may be considered the "best" of the collection. It is again the theme of loss of innocence, as in "Las dos Elenas," but it is presented much more effectively because there is no doubt about the point of view and the narrator is the "victim" himself, rather than the double-dealing adulterer. In other words, there is more inner consistency and no attempt to mystify the reader by too many implications. This time the presentation is truly more straightforward and amorality is again seen to be more "innocent," more honest, than the "old morality" of the title. Although now the old morality is not presented as decadent (implied in the adultery of Victor and his mother-in-law) so much as a form of ignorance—psychological ignorance, tortured into perversion and incestuous outlet because of an unreasoning adherence to the old hypocritical, priest-ridden "ethics" of Mexican Catholicism.

The attack on the priests and their hypocrisy, as a matter of fact, is the very keynote of the story. It is stated at once, with the opening words: ¡ *Zopilotes negros*! ¡ *Cuervos devoradores*! (Black buzzards! Ruinous crows!). Thus the old grandfather, shaking his cane angrily, insults the seminarians who pass his house, threatening to set the dogs on them. Of course, grandfather does all this theatrically, with his arm around his young concubine, Micaela, with whom he lives openly and whom he flaunts in the priests' faces. The narrator is a boy of thirteen who lives with his grandfather and Micaela and worships the old man in his uncompromising honesty. But the boy's aunts, who live nearby in the city (Morelia), are scandalized by the exposure of this youngster to the demoralizing influence of such a household. This environment, which the aunts see as vicious, is presented skillfully from the boy's point of view as one of bucolic innocence, of farm activities, vastly to the liking of the boy who is not in the least troubled by the situation that so disturbs his aunts. It is a hearty life, full of good food and play, undisturbed sleep, and no complications about sex.

Inevitably the aunts arrive, with a writ from the court that has jurisdiction over minors, to "rescue" Alberto, the boy, from the moral squalor in which he lives. The interview between the grandfather and the aunts is in Fuentes' best style, rapid, deadly, deeply ironic. In a paragraph we "see" the three aunts, one with a tic of the eye, the second with a wig that slips, and the third, the unmarried aunt, Benedicta, always dabbing at her nose with her black-lace hankie. The dialogue is economical but most effective—the three aunts firing off their condemnations like hysterical old pea-shooters, brandishing their writ. They win, and carry off Alberto to be "properly" brought up in the house of Aunt Benedicta.

Fuentes presents her in a not unkindly fashion. She is the real victim of the old morality because it is her character that has been twisted and warped by this hysterical adherence to a hypocritical creed. She is not even aware herself of the primitive physical, biologic forces that propel her to seduce her nephew. She is thirty-four, he is now fourteen, a juicy young man who by his very presence, his propinquity, his physical animality, actually seduces her, although he is not aware of this either. It is part of Fuentes' art that he presents all this to the reader indirectly, subtly, through the actions and reactions of the two protagonists who act out their inevitable comedy in the big, old-fashioned house. Speaking of Micaela, the grandfather's cook-concubine, Alberto repeats what his grandfather has said: "Naturally, they sleep together. Grandfather says that a man should never sleep alone or he'll dry up, and a woman the same."[8] This statement upsets the aunt out of all proportion and she stops bothering the boy for the rest of the day. All is not unrelieved psychological sordidness, however. Fuentes develops the boy's character skillfully showing, through his changing interests, how he, the boy, is changing from an unaware thirteen-year-old into a pubescent, sexually ready fourteen-year-old, still with some little-boy reactions, not yet a man—the incident of the captured lizard, which he gives to his aunt with all a little-boy's eagerness, and which becomes subtly symbolic of the boy himself as the palpitating body of the little reptile fills her hand. The whole story is consistently and convincingly presented from the boys's point of view, from the sequence of the mutual seduction to the end, at which point the boy is his aunt's little lover. He is, naturally, somewhat confused at the end and he somehow feels that back at the ranch, with his grandfather, there was *más moralidad* (more morality).

This is a delicate theme to handle and even more delicate to present without slipping into bathos. At the end he almost does, but Fuentes avoids it because all the way through the story the boy's character and its development have been consistent and convincing. He is an innocent child even though he has accepted a conventionally shocking solution to the aunt's problem. Again, this is a fairy tale seen through the horrifying glass: Tom Sawyer gone wrong with a lecherous Aunt Polly. But it is not pornographic, unless sensuality itself, the innocent sensuality of a young animal, or even the smothered, hysterical sensuality of an aging virgin, be so considered.

On the basis of our analyses so far, we can say that it is clear that Carlos Fuentes as a writer is more interested in character and character development than in any other aspect of the novelistic art. When we have done with our total view of his work, we shall see that he is not really interested in plot in any sense of the word. "Plot," even in the modern view of it as a "progression," in Fuentes is simply contributory to the presentation of a fascinating character. The situation in which the character develops may be realistic or fantastical, but it is essential only to the unfolding of the observed figure as such. Fuentes is a peoplewatcher and he populates his books and his tales with existential, even Surrealistic, characters who react convincingly in the situations, largely naturalistic, that he contrives for them.

The three remaining stories of this collection do not merit such close attention as the one we have just discussed. The fifth, "El costo de la vida," with its ironic title ("The Cost of Life"), is one of the author's sociological comments on life. A young school-teacher, trying to make his union an effective and truly representative instrument for bettering the conditions of life for himself and for his fellow teachers, is cynically murdered by the local union bosses who prefer to keep the instrument in their own hands as a source of income and power. Once more the "innocent," who naively thought he could do something against the age-old forces (in this case disguised as union leaders and not as Aztec gods) of evil and corruption, is destroyed. Prometheus never wins, not because he is not really Prometheus, not even because he is a naive little fool, but because by the very nature of things he cannot win. This pessimistic despair is by and large only an aesthetic attitude on Fuentes' part, not an innate world view. In his own life he betrays little of this aesthetic despair which he eliminates by projecting it into his work.

"Un alma pura" ("A Pure Soul"), the sixth story, is a touching tale of star-crossed lovers, lost through the complications of their own neuroses rather than through any circumstantial forces inimical to the fulfillment of their love. It is fulfilled and ends in disillusion and ennui, a variation on the French idea that the opposite of love is not hate but indifference. The story is ably told and we are sorry for the lovers but we do not feel really involved in their inevitable misfortune since it is obvious almost from the beginning that their creator intends to destroy them. The fact that their love ends in death is also incidental since, in any case, the heart must die before the body, and once the heart has stopped the rest is unimportant. Fuentes is very skillful in his handling of the presentation—the international ambience, the vocabulary evocative of mood, the nostalgic air—but the characters in this case do not really live, he has lost them in the clouds of fantasy which surround them. One might say that there is a quality of lyrical unreality that invests the whole story, but somehow it does not quite come off. Juan Luis never really touches us, Claire is too misty to be real.

The seventh and last tale, "A la víbora de la mar" ("To the Sea Serpent"), is an unrelieved study in evil, in which two homo-

sexuals, partners, fleece women on transatlantic liners by pretending to be in love with them until they get their money. Isabel,
the victim, is the innocent, aging (thirty-seven-year-old) virgin
who, in her ignorance of the world (again that Fuentian combination), is driven to suicide when she accidentally discovers
the relationship of her "husband" with his lover. The whole company of the ship, from the bartender to the passengers, is evil—
not a ship of fools but of devils—and Isabel moves among them
condemned to destruction from the beginning. The story is depressing and one seeks diversion in the details: the name of the
"husband," Harrison Beatle (with mischievous humor, Fuentes
makes him a Philadelphian); the fact that this evil ship is British;
the young adventurer is a Seventh-day Adventist. The story is, in
fact, so heavy that one is inclined to think that Fuentes cannot be
serious; he has written it with his tongue in his cheek. But if so,
he spoofs everything, even himself, since after all he *is* telling the
story. We cannot even take Isabel's suicide seriously. Nobody can
be that naive. He is putting us on, pulling the reader's leg, providing a tale of unrelieved evil for the titillation of the bourgeoisie. He must be aware that most of his readers will "catch
on." This story illustrates, perhaps better than any other, what may
be called, for lack of a better adjective, the mischievous element
in Fuentes. An occasional spoof may be allowed him—in general
he has given good value in this collection.

We have said enough about the short stories to whet the ap-
petite for a consideration of the more important genre in the
work of Carlos Fuentes. First and last he is a novelist, he thinks
like a novelist, he writes like one—let us inspect his novels.

CHAPTER 8

The Novels

THE international reputation of Carlos Fuentes rests almost entirely on his novels, four of which (so far) have been published in English in the United States. If four novels are enough on which to base such a reputation then, from a critical point of view, they must be remarkable indeed; otherwise one suspects that some of the *réclame* may be due to the high-pressure marketing techniques of modern publishers.

The fact that the novels of Carlos Fuentes are selling does not necessarily mean that they are worth buying. To a certain extent, his work, like that of many foreign writers, is selling because the publishing business has "discovered" that there is a market for good translations. As a consequence, we are in the midst of what Emir Rodríguez Monegal calls, in the history of Western literature, "a quiet but thorough revolution."[1] There is great international activity among writers, publishers, and editors; meetings of publishers' associations (all of which have international connections), meetings of editors who are members of juries of international prize-awarding bodies, meetings of writers themselves in P.E.N. conventions and other professional congresses. All of this activity has basically two purposes: to foster the exchange of ideas and to promote the sale of the authors' works. Few authors, certainly not Fuentes, object to this double purpose; few object to being considered "pundits," and likewise few object to promoting the sale of their books. The only questionable aspect of the whole campaign—because it is a campaign—is the tacit establishing and acceptance of certain artificial values: a work must potentially be a "best seller," otherwise the hapless author will be cast back into his provincial dungeon, his local market, where (even there) his sales will suffer because of his "failure"in the international market. This obviously has very little to do with his talent as a writer—Ortega y Gasset warned us as long ago as 1932 of the danger of applying democracy (mass acceptance or mass rejection) to art. Therefore the independent critic is also faced with a double problem: he must as honestly as possible evaluate the work under consideration on aesthetic grounds, and yet, in doing so, he must deal with a work that has already been hailed as a "masterpiece" by reviewers and by large advertisements.

We have to give some thought to all this since it has been said, sarcastically, of Fuentes that "he is the very model of a modern major novelist."[2] And according to his publishers, the sale of his works in translation has been "quite satisfactory."[3] Hence we need be on our guard as to whether or not the announced "fact" of excellence is merely the result of what another critic has called, in connection with the whole campaign of international promotion, a "game of mirrors face to face."[4] In short, what we do have to worry about is deciding whether the reputation is deserved, and if so, why.

The six novels that Carlos Fuentes has written and published to date are the following, *La región más transparente,* first published in Mexico in 1958 (internal evidence indicates that parts of it were written as early as 1951) and published in 1960 in the United States under the title of *Where the Air Is Clear.* The second, *Las buenas consciencias,* was published in Mexico in 1959 and in the United States in 1961, with the English title of *The Good Conscience.* The third, and to date the one that has received most attention, is *La muerte de Artemio Cruz,* published in Mexico in 1962 and in the United States in 1964 as *The Death of Artemio Cruz.* His fourth work, *Aura,* was published in Mexico in 1962; it has been translated into English but not yet published. The fifth, *Zona sagrada,* was published in Mexico in 1967 and is as yet untranslated; the title is a pun, it means both "Home Base," in a child's game, and "Sacred Zone" or "Sacred Area," in a theological sense. And the sixth, which won the Seix Barral Prize in Barcelona, is *Cambo de piel,* published in Mexico in 1967, and called *Change of Skin* in the English translation, published in 1968.

There is a great deal of importance to a first novel. It is, in effect, a young author's declaration, his throwing down of the gauntlet, his statement. Generally, he is most self-revealing in the first novel, he is presenting himself before he has become a wily old professional. Very often it will be revealing in the sense that it contains in embryo much of the thought and style of presentation that will be developed in later work. Also very often it will be less well-organized, less focussed, than subsequent work. The young author in his first unveiling has so much to say, he spills it all out, he does indeed suffer from logorrhea, and, as a consequence, usually the second novel is correspondingly meager. All of this is true in the case of the first and second novels of Carlos Fuentes. The first work runs to 376 pages, the second to 148; the first is a chaotic panorama of more than a score of "types" in modern Mexico City, the second concentrates on a single youthful rebel in a provincial capital; the first is diffuse and yet powerful, the second is focussed and therefore powerful; the first combines many techniques, the second is more traditionally narrative. Let us take a look at the first.

I   La región más transparente (Where the Air Is Clear)

The title is a quotation from the work of Alfonso Reyes (see Footnotes 4 and 11, Chapter 1) and refers to Anáhuac—the valley of Mexico—as a region where the air is clear. Indeed, it used to be such a region, before the drying up of Lake Texcoco and modern industrialization brought dust and smog, changing what was once a high, healthy tableland of a relatively low population density into an overcrowded metropolis with air pollution. When Fuentes chose this title, he was an admirer and disciple of Reyes. As writers, they are worlds apart, and as men also. However, Reyes (1889-1959) was the unofficial guide and teacher of a whole generation of younger Mexicans, not so much in style and philosophy but simply as a father-figure, an image they could venerate. He was so erudite, so serene, so productive, and he had overcome the unfortunate involvement of his father in the overthrow of Madero. He was the intellectual par excellence and as such could serve as a rallying point for other intellectuals. Fuentes, consciously or unconsciously, like many young Mexican in-

tellectuals in the late 1940's and early 1950's, needed a respected
older intellectual, aloof, full of probity, whom he could admire,
even though he might disagree with much of what Reyes stood
for. All these young men learned much from Reyes in their need
to justify Mexico to themselves and themselves to Mexico.[5]

Where the Air Is Clear does not lend itself to brief summary;
in essence it is a kaleidoscopic presentation, in many vignettes, of
the quality of contemporary life in Mexico City. In reading this
work, one can particularly understand Fuentes' struggle to reconcile himself to the history of his country, and one cannot understand it unless one is more or less familiar with the events outlined in the first few chapters of this essay. He says many things
about Mexico, through the mouths of his characters, that he himself thought and felt and needed to analyze. For example, very
early in the novel (p. 21), he calls Mexico ". . . the saddest un-
happiest fleabitten land in the world"; and with respect to the
fact of *mestizaje,* which we have also insisted on in previous
chapters, he puts a long disquisition (pp. 44-48) into the mind
of Manuel Zamacona, the poet, on the need to "know what our
origin is."[6] This meditation is much more than simply a questioning about origins, it is also a questioning as to possible directions, about *becoming* original somehow out of *mestizo* origins.
And the question further is ". . . what is the true model, the true
form. . . . Which should he himself *imitate?* (p. 45, italics ours).
In other words, one becomes original *by* imitation—not a modern
idea but still a dangerous one: it seems just as likely that one
becomes imitative by imitation. There is much more in a similar
vein; political directions are also touched on. But the mimetic
quality of Mexican life is most important to Fuentes. Much further on (p. 218), the same character, Manuel Zamacona, discussing the country's needs with the banker Federico Robles, insists
that Mexicans have always aped foreigners, in clothes, in attitudes, in mummery—but he extenuates the statement by attribut-
ing the new awareness of this mimetism to the liberating effect
of the Revolution: ". . . without the Revolution, we would never
have faced the problem of Mexico's meaning, its past" (p. 219).
But Robles has previously already decided, and declared, that this
self-recognition is the new tyranny that has replaced the old: "Today no one tyrannizes Mexicans. They don't need to. Mexicans

are tyrannized by what they are. And for thirty years there has been no other tyranny" (p. 88). He points out that "the instinct of the country" is inevitably toward bourgeois stability, that Calles "laid the foundation [and] Cárdenas brought it to life. . ." (p. 89). All of these thoughts are Fuentes' own, his attempt to come to some sort of grips with what Mexico was and then, because of the Revolution, became.

But the novel is not just a frame for Fuentes' own theorizing about the origins, identity, or directions of the *mestizo;* it is also an ambitious and largely successful attempt to do for Mexico City what John Dos Passos did for New York in *Manhattan Transfer.* Fuentes takes the profession of novelist seriously, he studies techniques and styles and applies what he has learned in his own work. Like most eclectics, he occasionally combines incongruous elements of style, or even deliberately uses the technique of abrupt contrasts too often or too heavily. For example, after every heavily emotional scene—the breakup of Norma Laragoiti's marriage to the banker Robles, a veritable *Götterdamerung* of bourgeois vulgarity, with overturned furniture, smashed vases, and finally a burning house in which Norma perishes—there is juxtasposed a scene in a discordant minor key, in which the obverse of the social coin, the "poor" side, offers an identical emotional release which borders on the grotesque: the death of Gabriel, the wetback, in a low, cheap "dive." This sort of writing is dangerous in that occasionally the contrast offered is too incongruous, it does not come off, and we get not a switch from major to minor but simply a *reductio ad absurdum* of the original emotionally overcharged scene. It is all very well for an author to claim later that all this is done deliberately; that life, after all, offers many notable examples of the ridiculously incongruous, of the grotesque distortion, and that he is simply selecting. Life does not offer these transitions symmetrically, life does not observe the dramatic need for catharsis, or offer convenient occasions for release from overwrought emotional crisis.

The work is divided into three parts, neither even nor equal in importance or intent. The orchestration is certainly not symphonic, though it might be said that the intent of the work as a whole is—the presentation of the City, through a combination of many moods, divided into three parts, is a sort of psychological symphony. Each part in turn is subdivided into what in an old-fashioned novel would be chapters, here sections, each with its indicative title, generally the name of the character who provides the point of view for that section, although occasionally a symbolic title is preferred ("Navel of the Moon," "City of Palaces," "Eagle Being Animate," etc.). The style is an eclectic combination of Aldous Huxlesy (*Point Counterpoint*), John Dos Passos (*Manhattan Transfer, USA*), James Joyce (*Ulysses*), and Fuentes. The Fuentian element is chiefly the *milieu*, the setting, both philosophical and psychological. The symmetry of presentation, though irregular, is apparent—we start with a party at Bobó's, and end with a party at Bobó's, surrounded by the same vain, silly, useless people, minus a few who have died. The novel ends with a peroration to the "Lords of night . . . lords of life" (Mother Mexico?) in what is apparently again an attempt to exorcise the old Aztec gods that rule the land. That they do rule is clearly one of the author's theses, made obvious in the character of Teódula Moctezuma, the old *curandera* (healing woman), who haunts the scene like the Witch of Endor, with the journalist, Ixca Cienfuegos, playing the part of a Mexican Saul.

Ixca as Saul, however, is not convincing—he leads no one to anything save death and destruction, finally causing his own death and that of another character, Rodrigo Pola, in a deliberately contrived automobile accident. This is another thesis of the author's—in imitating the foreigner, the *mestizo* even apes the foreign myths and gets them all mixed up with his own myths, especially mixing up the Christian idea of sacrifice with the Aztec idea of blood sacrifice, in particular that of the hideous god Huichilobos. Every one of the principal characters is sacrificed to some aspect or other of myth—the myth of bourgeois stability in the case of the banker Robles, the myth of the bitch-goddess Success in the case of the poet-turned-scenarist Rodrigo Pola, the myth Look-Out-For-Number-One in the case of Norma Larragoiti, the myth of the Keen Intellectual in the case of Manuel Zamacona (who dies by the pistol of a deadly drunk while trying to buy gas to escape from Acapulco)—all myths, the author shows, all of them false, all equally deadly, all projections of our own desires. It is a large, generously populated book—populated by rascals, not one redeemed by any saving virtue, not even the

blind Hortensia Chacón, who has abandoned her petty function-
ary of a husband because he is too petty to "understand" her; her
blindness, which her husband caused, does not ennoble her, she
is simply portentously symbolic of frustration and defeat turned
into a useless groping toward fulfillment.

What then is the value of this hyper-charged canvas, filled with
vain, superficial, stupid fools? It has the value of some of those
enormously crowded Surrealistic canvasses of Hieronymus Bosch,
filled with disgusting little diabolic figures breaking wind. Why
does an artist see life or his world in such a guise? No one can
answer that, not even the artist. That is the way he sees it at that
particular stage of his development—another term for his own
passage through life, his own reaction to time and transition.
Fuentes presents many, many facets of life here—all, in one way
or another, a reflection of the impact of the Revolution on the city
and its people: there is nostalgia for the pre-Revolution Mexico
City, the City of Palaces that was orderly and reasonable, of the
times of Don Porfirio (that is another of the themes, nothing is
"reasonable" anymore); there is the impact of betrayal and fear
in the death of Gervasio Pola, father of the poet Rodrigo, who
leaves his wife and dies facing the firing squad, with the three
companions he has betrayed (his wife, much later, in a moment
of bitter truth, says, "Your father was a coward who betrayed his
comrades and died like a fool, leaving us in poverty." [p. 109]);
there is the somewhat inhuman curiosity of Ixca Cienfuegos who,
like a clinical journalist, takes a sadistic delight in trying to make
people face the truth about themselves; and through it all, there
is the brutal presentation of a thoroughly meretricious society,
mestizo and rootless because it does not know which are its roots.
And finally even that question, posed by the author himself—the
origin and identity of Mexico—is tossed into the cauldron along
with everything else, and it too is futile, equally unanswerable,
and we are left with the final statement, at the end of the peroration, in the mind of Gladys García, the dance-hall whore, who
somehow symbolizes the whole city: "Here we bide. What are
we going to do about it? Where the Air Is clear" (p. 376).

There are insights that justify much of the verbiage. "Sometimes immensity does not make men little" (p. 54), expressing
the feeling of Gervasio Pola as he leads his companions into the

high sierra after escaping from the Federal prison. " . . . All
truth is measured by our own days and falls into a thousand fragments in the light of every glance, every heartbeat . . ." (p. 175),
expressing the rationalization of one of the Díaz aristocrats,
analyzing the past. As a writer, Rodrigo Pola justifies his acceptance of "Success" by commenting on the intangibility of writing;
"No matter how tangible a book is, to see, smell, or touch it does
not prove anything or say anything about its stylistic excellence.
. . . It is so hard to apprehend the intrinsic being" (p. 191). On
God: "For if God is infinite good . . . He is also infinite evil . . ."
(p. 205), states Ixca in one of his more Aztec moods, a thought
he amplifies a little further on in the same conversation by stating
that God is not one but many. Insights, in the hands of an intellectual, can so easily degenerate into insults—Rodrigo feels in-
sulted by Ixca's nonsense.

Apart from the large stylistic influences already noted, of Huxley, Dos Passos, Joyce, we can also see a great deal of more specifically stylistic influence from Azuela, particularly from *La luciérnaga* (The Firefly). Azuela himself states that he wrote *La
luciérnaga* (as well as *La malhora* and *El desquite* [*The Getting-
even*]) in order to force respectful attention from the literary
critics who were slow in according him recognition. What he did
in jest, however, achieved its purpose and critical acclaim was
immediately forthcoming. It has consequently been held by some
scholars (Manuel Pedro González, F. Rand Morton) that we
need not take the "Cubistic" style of these works seriously; others
(Torres-Rioseco, Jefferson Spell) feel equally that these works
must be taken for what they are: projections in prose of a Picas-
so-like style. The opinion of the latter critics seems to have pre-
vailed and these works are now accepted as contributions that
must be taken seriously in spite of the leg-pulling intent, as productions of a mature and talented writer who, knowing he was as
good a writer as many who had already won recognition, decided
to conquer the field on its own grounds, so to speak, and did so
triumphantly. Azuela was amused by the furor and satisfied with
the results. Similarly, Fuentes, in this work, shows that he is mature enough to profit by the experience of others and to present
the critics with the sort of thing they delight in—a stylistically
ambitious panorama of modern society. And the so-called "Cubis-

tic" elements are there too: the dreams (pp. 161-62), the syncopation in Norma's mind after she has escaped from drowning but thinks she has drowned her lover (pp. 261-62), the general use of synesthesia in presenting the garish neon colors of Mexico City by night as seen by Gladys García or Gabriel the wetback.

To a certain extent, what we have said is that *Where the Air Is Clear* is a contrived book, an artificial elaboration, modelled deliberately on successful predecessors. It is, but we do not say so in condemnation. If, as Fuentes states, the road to originality is through imitation, then we must allow him his experiment, especially as, by and large, it is a well-done, convincing experiment. One may say that some of the characters are unreal, too symbolic, too puppet-like—in any panoramic presentation of life this is inevitable, some of the characters will be like those little Judas figures dancing on the end of a string in the street fairs of Mexico City on the Day of the Dead; and also inevitably much of the action in the panorama must seem like a wax-work *Todendanz*. This is all part of the "picture," and the very artificiality is part of the art, the contriving is part of the conviction that Life itself is a cunning artifice.

And finally, in order to appreciate and understand this book, one should have a knowledge of the facts of the Revolution. How is one to understand, for example, the early memories of the banker, Frederico Robles, when he was a peon on the land of Don Ignacio de Ovando, or the impulse to revolution given by the Río Blanco massacres, or the decision taken by many revolutionaries at Celaya—all recalled by Robles between pages 71 and 90? Let us not be provincial ourselves about this Revolution, made in Mexico by Mexicans for Mexicans—it has had as wide an impact throughout Latin America as ever the Russian revolution had on Europe. By and large, Fuentes has achieved the job he set himself in this, his first novel—he has indeed done for Mexico what Dos Passos did for New York and in doing so Fuentes has made Mexico City as much a part of the "cultural baggage" of the contemporary well-read man as was the Paris of Zola or the New York of Dos Passos. In view of this fact—perhaps even because of it—it is no longer so odd that Fuentes has now turned his own back on Mexico. By writing about it he has got it out of his system in that particular aspect; there are many other aspects, and he will never get them out of his system, but he must try, and in trying he produces interesting, readable books.

II   Las buenas conciencias (The Good Conscience)

This book is a biographical presentation, a lengthy character analysis, of a young man and his development in a provincial city, his rebellion against the life of his society and his final compromise and adjustment so as not to be crushed by that society. It is a novel written as a straightforward narrative, much more "traditional" in form than the first. The scene is a provincial city, Guanajuato, the cradle of Mexican liberty, the Philadelphia of Mexico, and in trying to recreate the atmosphere of Guanajuato, Fuentes himself declares that he felt he must write in the manner of Benito Pérez Galdós, the Spanish Balzac.[7] The protagonist of this work, Jaime Ceballos, has appeared briefly, towards the end, in *Where the Air Is Clear*, as the unsophisticated, provincial suitor of Betina Régules, the chic young debutante of Mexico City society. Now we are given a full-length portrait of this young man and his formation. He will appear again in *The Death of Artemio Cruz*, as an episodic figure, old, tired, and sophisticated at last. This carrying of the same character through several works, giving him his own full presentation in one of them, is in the great tradition of the nineteenth-century novel, that of Balzac as well as of Galdós. Originally Fuentes had the idea of making this novel the first of a tetralogy, again in the grand tradition of the great writers of the Golden Age of the novel, but he has apparently abandoned this idea.[8] In any event, *The Good Conscience* was undoubtedly an easier work to write, and it is certainly an easier one to read, than either the one that preceded it or the one that followed it.

The title in Spanish is in the plural, *Las buenas conciencias*, and conveys more of Fuentes' intention than the English title. It is not only the conscience of Jaime Ceballos that is under examination but that of the provincial society of Guanajuato itself as well. The subtitle might very well be "The Making of a Hypocrite." Fuentes' thesis is that the individual cannot accomplish anything by isolated rebellion against the norms of his society, that sooner or later he will be obliged to conform, forced to accept the social hypocrisies that he originally rejected. If he does not, he will be himself ejected, or he will have to remove himself to another milieu where he will have the freedom to live his own life. Many of us, however, do not have the strength to live our own lives, rejecting our so-called peers and rejected by them. Jaime Ceballos is unable to achieve that ultimate liberation and in his wanton killing of an affectionate cat he symbolizes his surrender, with loathing, to what his own character must now turn into: acceptance of whores instead of love, commerce instead of comrades. The killing of the cat is simply the confirmation of what he has already done in rejecting Father Obregón's plea for sincerity: lip service instead of God.

This is a short novel—148 pages—and yet we find in it all the information necessary to the delineation of the development of Jaime Ceballos' character. Of the total of ten chapters, the first two are given over to sketching for the reader the background of Jaime's family and we start at the beginning—with a presentation of Guanajuato itself. The city is recognizable, we are given enough information about it to differentiate it and its citizens from, let us say, Puebla, and yet actually it is nothing but a backdrop against which the development of Jaime is staged. And the tone is set at once: on the second page of the first chapter we are told categorically that 'The citizen of Guanajuato is . . . a practiced, talented, certified hypocrite,'[9] and this is clinched on the next page by the remark that ". . . in Guanajuato public relations have precedence over private truth." There is an attempt at Voltairean irony in these opening chapters and the reader wonders if here we are to meet a Mexican Candide. But eclectic as ever, Fuentes soon abandons the Voltairean attitude as he gets engrossed in the presentation of his story.

The early history of the family is given to us against the historical background, first of the Wars of Independence, then of the Díaz dictatorship, and finally of the Revolution itself, almost precisely one hundred years which turn the progeny of a draper from Madrid into a typical little Mexican bourgeois with pretensions of aristocracy. In the third chapter an acceptably Freudian cause is given for Jaime's ambivalence toward his family. His mother, an impossibly common woman, has been got rid of by the family, represented by the sister and brother-in-law of Jaime's father Rodolfo. When this precious pair return from England, where they have sat out the Revolution in safety, they reestablish themselves, like once-exiled monarchs, as heads of the clan, wresting control from the weak Rodolfo, whom they oblige to separate from his vulgar wife, annulling his marriage in fact if not in law. Asunción, the sister, has had no children, due to the sterility of her husband, Jorge Balcárcel, and she and her husband "adopt" little Jaime, not only by getting rid of his real mother but by preempting the role and relationship even of his real father, who is relegated to a little room on the roof, above the servants' quarters. The little boy naturally does not understand why his father and his "mamá Asunción" do not share the same room, while his Uncle Jorge, a rigid Victorian (or, in Mexico, a Diazian) hypocrite, does occupy the same bedroom. This Hamlet-like situation inevitably produces, on a tiny scale, the same sort of Hamletian reaction: frustration and an inability to act, which, in Jaime, expresses itself by an attempt to create his own world, in protest against the unacceptable world of his uncle and his aunt-mother.

Part of his protest is in the form of hyper-religiosity; he even dreams of becoming a priest. His withdrawal into this fantasy world eventually alarms his overseers who, with typical lack of understanding, simply tell him to stop having such a "mistaken idea about religion" (p. 33). This further frustration drives the growing boy into further withdrawal, now to that ultimate bastion of selfhood, and he begins to console himself with masturbation. After the emotional orgy of Holy Week and Easter, in a scene that Fuentes no doubt meant to be shocking, the boy even kneels in the empty church before the wounded body of the Savior and offers himself in this fashion to God. A culmination to this period in the development of the tormented adolescent is given by the episode of Ezequiel. A rebel miner who has run away from the punishments of the *cacique* (boss) takes refuge in the Balcárcel stable, one of Jaime's favorite retreats, and presses Jaime to help him. Jaime is romantically enamored of the idea and identifies with this strong, manly rebel, but in his efforts to help, he unwittingly betrays the man's hiding place to his suspicious uncle. The uncle of course has the miner arrested and Jaime sees him dragged off by the police. The traumatic effect on young Jaime is tremendous and he runs after the marching men, shouting "Ezequiel! It wasn't me! I swear, it wasn't me!" (p. 58)

Inevitably, young Jaime now hates his uncle and all he stands for even more than ever, and in Chapter 5 some of this "all" that Uncle Jorge Balcárcel stands for is presented. The characters now paraded before the reader are more real, less stereotyped, less symbolic, than the *caterva*, the macabre mob of grinning puppets that throng the background of *Where the Air Is Clear*. There are fewer and therefore they are presented in more detail. Some specifically stand out: Señorita Pascualina, the self-appointed guardian of morals, who skulks watchfully "in movies, at dances, even on the streets in the small hours of the morning" (p. 60), to see to it that young men and women do not approach each other unchastely; Father Lanzagorta "who barks his Sunday sermons and every Friday hungrily presents his greyhound profile at dinner" (pp. 59-60); Father Obregón who truly tries to help the boy but fails; and above all, his special friend, Juan Manuel Lorenzo, the pureblooded Indian, who also tries in his way to help Jaime free himself from the bourgeois vise in which he finds himself. Juan Manuel is more than just an incidental character; he is a school friend of Jaime's and has more influence on him than anyone else. He too fails to liberate Jaime, but the failure is really Jaime's, who does not really want to free himself but wants rather to make Uncle Jorge, Aunt-Mother Asunción, his real father Rodolfo, his whole society, in short, behave as he prefers; to change them, not to turn his back on them. When, in the end, he finds that they and their society are stronger than he is, he turns his back on Juan Manuel and says good-bye to what his friend stands for, and finally joins the middle-class society he condemned.

But before this dénouement is reached there are many experiences through which Jaime must move before he reaches the point of resolution. Chapter 6, which is the longest section of the biography, carries us to the decisive point in Jaime's development. Through his friendship with Juan Manuel he goes to a laborers' bar one afternoon and there, with two whores, he sees his real mother for the first and only time. And when he realizes who the dark, gray-haired woman with "the sad, defensive eyes" is (p. 96), he cannot stay nor can he make himself known to her—he leaves the bar abruptly. Later on we learn that Juan Manuel had taken his friend to this bar so that he might have the opportunity to meet and acknowledge his mother and when Jaime flees, unable to identify himself to the woman, Juan Manuel knows that Jaime is posturing in all his attitudes and that he will never liberate himself from the bourgeois society of which he is, basically, a part.

The chief result of this rejection of his mother, of his betrayal of the "common" element in his makeup, is that he wanders in an orgy of guilt out of the city and indulges in self-flagellation. When he finally staggers "home," he is on the point of collapse, and in fact does collapse and lies sick for some time. It is in Chapter 7 that he tries to reconcile his many conflicts through the help of Father Obregón, but it is evident that even at this point of crisis he prefers his posturing and sees himself as a martyr heaping coals of remorse on the heads of his foster parents, Jorge and Asunción.

But his real father, Rodolfo, must still be exorcised and, in Chapter 8, the old man sickens and, after a long period of suffering, dies of cancer of the stomach. All through his last, mortal illness, he tries to reconcile his son to himself, makes groping gestures of sorrow, reaches out in lonely pleading for his son's forgiveness. But Jaime cannot bring himself to respond to his father's pathetic offers, he hardens his heart, he rejects his father even more emphatically than he rejected his mother—he fled from her, but he turns his back coldly and remorselessly on his father. And he watches his father die without responding to the outstretched hand, without meeting the pleading eyes. This is almost the final factor in the making of Jaime's conscience, in the molding of his conscience to the image of those of his society, of that of his uncle, of his aunt, of Señorita Pascualina, of Father Lanzagorta, the Holy Name Society, the Party Youth organizations, all the hollow, empty shells that form the mask a man must wear when there is nothing inside. The final episode is that of his visit to the house of prostitution. Inevitably he picks the same "short brown-skinned girl with a mole on her forehead" (p. 135) that his father used to visit before his death. And at the whorehouse he sees his Uncle Jorge Balcárcel, a drunken clown, ". . . dancing all alone with a bottle of rum hugged in his arms" (p. 134).

There is one more scene with Father Obregón, in which he now rejects that good man's exhortation to save himself through love. Jaime's damnation, or—from the social point of view—his salvation, is now complete. "Who was Obregón [he thinks to himself] to talk to him like this? Cassocked eunuch . . . who did not know true male passions" (p. 139). Jaime makes his final confession to himself, since he will never again make a sincere confession to a priest, before the same image of Christ to which he had offered his adolescent self-abuse, and then "the voice of Christ faded . . ." (p. 140) and Jaime achieves the peace of conformity. He has accepted himself for what he is, a little bourgeois hypocrite, and, very well, that is what he will be. There is one last reaction of his wounded soul, the death of the cat, previously mentioned, and with that he purges himself of all desire, or need, to be anything but what he is; a Ceballos of Guanajuato, a righteous man, with a good conscience.

Fuentes has admitted that there is much that is autobiographical in this small volume on the making of a hypocrite, that he is in effect exorcising his own past.[10] This is not to say, by any means, that the details of the narrative are autobiographical as such. His own background and upbringing are quite different, as we have seen in Chapter 6. However, he is talking about the forces of conformity and the rebellion of any young middle-class Mexican who, in the 1940's, was trying to understand his own origins and environment. The pressures of society will be much the same in any milieu since they are a product, in Fuentes' social theory, of the class to which the individual belongs. They may seem more concentrated in the provincial city of the novel, since the sphere of action is more restricted, and hence they may seem also more malevolent and inescapable than would similar pressures in a world capital such as Washington or Rome or Mexico City; but basically they are the same pressures to conform, essentially the same attempts to make the young individual accommodate himself to the social pattern as those suffered by Jaime Ceballos.

There are many influences apparent in this novel. Those mentioned of Galdós and Balzac are evident in the style and traditional form of presentation. There is also a comparison to be made between this story and that told by José Rubén Romero in

Mi caballo, mi perro y mi rifle (mentioned in Chapter 3). Fuentes is quite a different sort of man from Romero, he does not have
Romero's *don de gentes* (gift of getting along with people, of
making people like him), but he is just as concerned with social
justice and with what individual liberty means as was Romero
in his time. He does not have Romero's humor. Actually what
little humor there is in Fuentes is ironic, biting, sarcastic, very
rarely what we would call good-humored. This truly deep difference in the personality of the two writers is due basically to their
different vision of the world. Romero's humor (in *Pito Pérez,* his
best-known work, for example) can indeed be ironic and equally
as biting a commentary on the society of his time; but there is
always a wry quality of self-mockery which is not present at all
in Fuentes. So the similarities between Jaime Ceballos and Julián
Osorio, the protagonist of *Mi caballo . . .*, are superficially very
striking but the way in which the two men resolve their conflict
and the difficulties arising from it are quite distinct. Julián Osorio
escapes from a contemptible life into an heroic one as the Revolution affords him the opportunity to save himself from the psychological suffocation threatened by the weight of the hypocrisy
of family pretensions; Jaime Ceballos does not escape but re-
conciles himself to the contemptible life of the comfortable bourgeois. One may say that Jaime did not have the opportunity that
the Revolution offered to Julián, he is of a younger generation in
a more stable society. But we have seen that basically he does not
escape because he does not want to escape: since he cannot
change the family, he accepts the weight of the hypocrisy of its
pretensions, he ends by embracing all that he rebelled against.

And again Fuentes is presenting the nightmare—the dream he
dreamt that might have been. He himself escaped by becoming
a writer, a political extremist, and a bohemian (albeit a comfortable bohemian), turning his back on the (to him) stultifying
life offered in diplomatic society. The hero's name is unimportant, whether it be Julián Osorio or Jaime Ceballos, since actually
it is Fuentes or Romero who is projecting his own possibilities,
his own conflicts, his own rebellions in fictitious guise against a
backdrop of his own devising. The fact that "escape" as such, and
even the conflict itself, is psychological rather than physical was
recognized much more quickly by Romero than it was by Fuen-

tes. Theoretically, of course, Fuentes has recognized it (no one could be such an admirer of Faulkner without realizing that one may live the life of a gentleman farmer in a small southern town, outwardly conforming, and yet lead an inner life of the widest, and wildest, possible psychological liberation), but in practice he is still escaping. This is a definitely psychological reaction—he himself has said that after a certain amount of time in Mexico he feels "closed in" and must get away.[11] Other Mexicans have reported the same feeling—is it the mountains, is it the relative smallness of the social circle, or is it an almost neurotic reaction to a world one does not wish to accept for one reason or another?

The style of this work offers no tricks and no problems. It is straightforward narrative and none of the devices that Fuentes employed in his first book (and brings into fuller development in *The Death of Artemio Cruz*) are in evidence here. They are not needed and, indeed, they would be out of place since coruscations of stylistic technique would ill become a work avowedly patterned after Galdós. Also we can see clearly and without stylistic obfuscations that Fuentes can tell an interesting story without embellishing it or without complications of effect. The action—the development of Jaime's character—is made clear through unabashed incident and episode and the protagonist's reactions must logically and psychologically stand or fall on that basis, in accord with the value of the incident evoking them. If *Where the Air Is Clear* is a heavily-populated, overcharged canvas, then *The Good Conscience* is lean and personal, and gains by being so. One is more touched by Jaime's struggles than by the problems of the artificial people in the neonglare of Mexico City in the first book. And the extent to which Jaime Ceballos is Fuentes' alterego is, of course, strictly limited to the psychological realm, but adds spice to the interest that the incidents and episodes themselves legitimately awaken. It is, all in all, a thoroughly satisfactory novel in the Galdosian tradition, and the author even shows quite a bit of the master's ability to sketch incidental character deftly and convincingly. In this book Fuentes establishes himself as a real writer, to his own satisfaction, and he now feels free to go on to develop the technique that so intrigued him in his first novel, applying it now not to a multitudinous scene but concentrating it on the character of one man, Artemio Cruz.

III   La muerte de Artemio Cruz

(The Death of Artemio Cruz)

The experiment that Fuentes tried, on the whole successfully, in *Where the Air Is Clear*, he brings to triumphant mastery in *The Death of Artemio Cruz*. All the technical devices of style—stream-of-consciousness, flashbacks and flash-forwards, run-on sentences, association, symbolism, the subconscious—the works—he applies here not to a city and its life but to an individual and his death. The man's whole life is presented to us as a retrospective during the last twelve hours of his life, the twelve hours of his death throes, during which he recapitulates his whole existence prior to his agony. Naturally such an immense retrospective cannot be presented in orderly or chronological fashion: realism of presentation demands intermittence, juxtapositions, overlapping, and all the rest of the apparatus that the strange workings of a man's subconscious processes would impose. And realism of content demands that the author be free to present these episodes out of chronological order, as well as in the subtly varying styles that will convey an authentic impression of recollection by the mind of the dying man of the different stages and eras through which his life has passed: the immediate dying Artemio, the youthful Artemio, the ruthless, successful Artemio, the mature, the lusty-in-love Artemio, and so on.

And even more than this, the work is a combination of the technique of *Where the Air Is Clear* and the point of view (much amplified of course) of *The Good Conscience*. It is as though Fuentes had deliberately set out to prepare himself for the writing of this book by first trying his hand at the style he felt most appropriate and then setting himself to the psychological reconstruction of an individual, and then combining the two, the technique and the point of view, into one splendid opus. To a certain extent this is true. Fuentes originally had in mind the production of a tetralogy in which precisely such a total effect due to different styles and points of view would be sought. Although he seems to have abandoned this project, nevertheless some vestigial traces of the original intent are still to be detected. Published in Mexico in 1962 and in the United States in 1964, *The Death of Artemio Cruz* was received almost at once by almost all critics as a work worthy of high consideration and acclaim. And upon a first reading, one can understand why. It is almost the first work in this stylistic genre to be published in Mexico by an author writing in Spanish, although Fuentes himself had certainly given warning in his own first novel. If the critics did not take that first novel as seriously as they ought, or Fuentes himself as seriously as they ought, then they have no one but themselves to blame if the impact of this third book caught them unprepared. Most of them reacted favorably, stunned, one might say, by the frontal assault that this book makes on almost everything Mexican. We are talking now of the Mexican critics, of course. Adjectives such as "forceful;" "harsh," "unrelenting" (*despiadado*), even "overwhelming," were freely used in appraising the work. The United States critics were almost equally favorable, although one or two had reservations. Charles Poore, in the New York Times, for example, says that the many stylistic changes cause "reading troubles." But on the whole, his appraisal is laudatory: in the last paragraph of his review he handsomely acknowledges that "Unamuno's 'tragic sense of life' is brilliantly reflected in this novel," and that "it transcends its setting," that it gives us "a strangely oblique view of one man's Mexico."[12]

Another critic, Keith Botsford, is much less kind. As a matter of fact, he condemns the whole work as "insincere writing" (in the article previously mentioned above, in Footnote 2). But the fact remains that the book has been on the whole very well received and has been translated into the major European languages. The Italian critic, Giuseppe Tedeschi, calls it "an intense, strong work by a writer of high quality."[13] There is no question that it has aroused a certain amount of controversy, some of it rather bitter. In order to understand either the praise or the condemnation before considering further the critics' dicta, let us look at the book itself.

The twelve hours of his dying that provide Artemio Cruz with the occasion and the desperate need to review his own life are dealt with in over three hundred pages. It is obvious that in such an extensive treatment, much more must be dealt with than simply this one life. Indeed, we must meet in some detail his wife Catalina, his father-in-law Don Gamaliel, his first love Regina, his daughter Teresa, and various assorted revolutionaries, business associates, and other characters incidental to his life. They are all seen primarily through his knowledge of them, although consistency of point of view is not maintained and the author does at times avail himself of the traditional omniscience of a nineteenth-century novelist to present action or details of character which the subject, Artemio Cruz, could not have known. From the point of view of construction, this inconsistency is sometimes intrusive, and the mechanics of the presentation, with arbitrary or no divisions between the actions of one set of characters and those of a different set, do indeed make for the difficulties in reading that Poore notes. This is a deliberate device on the part of the author, of course, to reproduce the way the subconscious operates in presenting memories and fragments of memories, but then to combine those fragments that are legitimately a product of the subconscious of Artemio Cruz with other bits that could not have been dredged up by his subconscious mind at all, and present them all jumbled, does seem to place an undue strain on the reader's attention.

The role of the subconscious in this work is of primary importance. It is, as Fuentes himself says, a sort of Virgil who guides him through the twelve circles of his own Inferno.[14] And in the narrative, the subconscious is indicated by the use of *tú* (thou)— the familiar form of address—by which Artemio Cruz naturally addresses himself, or his subconscious addresses him. This device is useful, since *él* (he)—the third person—can similarly be made to represent Artemio in the past, and *yo* (I) stands for Artemio in the present. All this involves a good deal of conscious cooperation on the part of the reader, since the reader's subconscious, alas, is not involved in the process of absorbing the work, and the fact that Fuentes requires this effort on the part of his readers is an indication that he is well on his way down the road to the *nouveau roman* in objective if not yet in actual commitment. Fuentes is well aware of this since he believes that at this point he is still within the Naturalistic fold and has not yet proceeded (let us avoid the invidious "progressed") to the almost hermetic condition of, say, Alain Robbe-Grillet, the French Objectivist. But in no sense is this a Naturalistic novel in the nineteenth-century meaning of the term. Fuentes feels that *his* type of Naturalism means an internal validity within the novelistic structure which is sustained and in turn, sustains the external validity (. . . *la tabla de realidad externa sólo tiene validez en función de la novela misma, y viceversa*).[15]

The book opens with *yo*, awake, feeling the cold contact of the urine bottle, his first conscious moment after his heart attack, the first day of death; and it ends with the extinction of *yo*, *tú* and *él*—especially *tú*, the subconscious, the inner, real *yo*, who ". . . is dying, has died, will die."[16] In between we follow the peripatetics of a self-formed man and his own self-deformation in his whole ruthless, unscrupulous struggle, not just for survival but for success, full bourgeois, material success such as the Ceballos wished for Jaime, in the neon nightmare of Revolution and omniverous city, the city of that transparent region where the air is no longer clear.

Occasionally, not consistently, the author gives the reader a small indication of the path by allowing a date as a heading for some of the sections into which the long narartive is divided. Just as an indication of this arbitrariness (which, let us not forget, is supposed to reflect the arbitrariness of the subconscious), let us look at the dates as they occur throughout the work. 1941 is the first—Cruz is an established tycoon, an industrialist with many interests, ruthless, strong, hard—a fuller, more fleshed-out development of the banker, Federico Robles, of *Where the Air is Clear*. Also we meet his wife and daughter—they are shopping in preparation for the daughter's wedding. The wife seems to be the typical, petulant, spoiled rich woman, a combination of two characters from the first novel—Norma Larragoiti, plus the aristocratic *venida a menos* (financially ruined) Pimpinela de Ovando who stomachs with distaste the new post-Revolution upstarts, but who, nevertheless, stomachs them. Catalina, Cruz's wife, was also a landowner's daughter who has been forced by her father to marry the then Captain Cruz, the peasant nobody who has "made good" in the Revolution and can restore the family fortunes. Cruz's daughter, Teresa, is very similar, again more fully presented, to the Betina Régules, society debutante, who marries Jaime Ceballos.

These are all characters we have met before, but now they are presented in depth and, let us admit it, the style of presentation is more effective than the straightforward Galdosian narrative of *The Good Conscience*. At least it is so to the modern reader, one who has been conditioned already by Joyce and Dos Passos and Faulkner and is willing to make the effort that Galdós or Balzac do not require. Perhaps in seventy-five or a hundred years this will seem as tiresomely old-fashioned to the reader of the future as do the Victorian novelists to many readers today. And still in the first section, the inevitable clash between Cruz and his wife because of her "pretensions" and his resentment of them is also presented. He believes that she has always felt superior to him, and, like a child, his *tú* has avenged itself for the slights he has fancied by infidelities, by neglect, by the same sort of withdrawal that Jaime Ceballos practiced on his father.

We go back to 1919—the last sputtering years of the warphase of the Revolution—and we learn that through his association with young Gonzalo Bernal, Catalina's brother, fighting quixotically on the "wrong" side, Cruz has conceived the idea of using the death of Gonzalo in order to meet Catalina, and deliberately marry her in order to achieve respectability of background for the career he plans for himself. It is in this section that we get a glimpse of the young Artemio as he appeared to Catalina, who at first was inclined to like him, romantically, as a close comrade of her brother's: "She could not avoid meeting his green eyes. He was not handsome. But the olive skin . . . the sinuous strength of his body, the sensual lips . . ." (pp. 41-42) all attracted her physically. The green eyes are his most impressive characteristic and form an important part of his personal magnetism, which permits him to impose himself successfully on aristocrat, peon, business associates. We are given some indication in this section, too, of Cruz's quite cynical maneuvers (cynical because they are the same maneuvers that the Revolution was fought to abolish) to start building his fortune by seizing and manipulating the land of the dispossessed owners; by deceiving and manipulating (just as the former owners had done, only now in the name of "agrarian reform") the peasants, some of whom, in order to profit also, lent themselves to his game. But in this section also, Catalina discovers that Artemio is anti-Catholic, an unbeliever, and furthermore she has had time to wonder why her brother was shot and Artemio, his cell mate and fellow captive, was not. She will obey her father and marry him, but her future actions are now precast; she will love him physically because her body is attracted to him, but she will loathe him socially because he has deliberately used her dead brother and now her to advance himself. (All this is told from Catalina's point of view—one cannot help but ask just how this squares with the neo-Naturalistic definition that Fuentes himself formulated, or how it is to be reconciled with the overall point of view of the novel itself).

Still in this section, Cruz begins his first speculations with the "gringo" businessmen he will first serve, then represent and finally stand equal with. Some of these characters are rather stereotyped, drawn from the image created by the Revolution of the "exploiters" who are not content simply to exploit but must also meddle—each despises the other and each is equally despicable, lackeys of imperialism, interested only in the almighty dollar. It is in the portrayal of these somewhat stereotyped characters that Fuentes most reveals his own ideological orientation. The section closes with *tú* concerned again with his own suffering.

Now we move to 1913, at the beginning of the protagonist's service in the revolutionary ranks, and we read the only episode in the book in which Artemio is really human—the episode of his first love, his true love, for the Indian maid Regina. We know nothing about her, but his love for her is real and idyllic, and she is killed by the Federalists in reprisal on the civilians of a village in which the revolutionaries had taken shelter. Some of the bitterness of the war comes through here, in very personal terms. Artemio learns of her death only after the battle in which he has been wounded (and in which he has behaved rather cowardly—only the confusion of battle makes his wound heroic rather than disgraceful). And the tragedy of the loss of Regina is enough to justify psychologically all the subsequent deformation of Artemio's character. He is truly shattered inside—he had truly loved her because she had truly loved him; he had rejoiced in her loveliness, and the few brief months of their love would now be

buried in his inner being, to be covered like the grain of sand in
the oyster, to produce not a pearl but a monstrous cancerous
growth, a carapace that would cover over all the young Artemio
had been, and which finally even he himself would not remember accurately anymore.

The next two sections, 1924 and 1927, are devoted to further-
ing the development of Cruz in his relationship with Catalina,
his wife, and to relating the progress of his career. In the first,
the relationship deteriorates, to mutual toleration, and Catalina
finally voices her reproach: "He died [her brother] and you are
here, full of life and profiting by his inheritance" (p. 111). In the
second, Artemio prospers, he enters politics, joins the government party, becomes a deputy. There is an interlude in which his
tortured subconscious shrieks obscenities, revelling in all the
possible variations that it can devise of the ultimate obscenity
(pp. 142-47).

There is a short flash-forward, to 1947, in which Artemio indulges in the expensive infidelities of an aging rich man, taking
a pretty young secretary to a resort, only to have her flirt with a
handsome young man and to overhear himself described by other
guests as the beast who is keeping beauty. There is also an interlude with *tú* in which he reproaches himself (and somehow
so does Catalina) for an accident that happened to his son Lorenzo.

Another flashback, to 1915, and we get the whole sordid story
of his survival at the expense of Gonzalo Bernal, Catalina's
brother. The fortunes of war make the whole betrayal plausible
and excusable, but the subconscious knows what sort of scoun-
drel one is, and this memory joins the other, of Regina, deep in
the scarred depths of his being, to fester and add to the self-
loathing with which he now sees himself and which he projects
onto his family. Artemio's subconscious, while reproaching him,
on a subtly different level also rejoices: they died, you survived,
you survived; and it cannot accept now or even believe that this
time it too will die.

1934, 1939—trips to Paris, to New York, affairs with foreign
women, with friends of his wife's; the death of his son Lorenzo
in the Spanish Civil War. Each year, each episode, each scar,
like another ring on the trunk of an aging tree, brings Artemio

nearer his own death. The *tú* interjects itself more frequently; cyanosis has set in. His wife and his daughter, seated at his bedside, watch him. His daughter is convinced almost up to the moment of his death that he is making believe, that he is not really sick, that it is just one more of his wily, nasty tricks to hurt them.

1955, a society interlude, impressionistic, quickly done, various figures dance across his memory, Jaime Ceballos and his wife Betina, old Régules the financier, Laura, his wife's friend and his mistress. But he cannot die without one more recollection of his childhood. He is back with his Uncle Lunero, the mulatto; they live by the sea, in the tropics, very poor—he remembers what Lunero told him, that he is the illegitimate son of a landowner and Lunero's sister, Isabel Cruz. And in the final recollection, 1889, he seems even to remember his birth; his subconscious, grovelling before its own extinction, retreats to that initial point of life itself, before it too finally dies.

So we have traced and retraced a man's existence: 1941, 1919, 1913, 1924-27, 1947, 1915, 1934-39, 1955, and 1889. It begins with omega and ends with alpha and in between we truly run the gamut of all that can destroy a man, all that life can and does inevitably bring and which just as inevitably kills, first the soul and then the body. With the one exception already noted—Catalina's intrusion into the narrative from her own point of view—the novel is remarkably well constructed, convincing, and moving. So much so that we note a characteristic that is new in Fuentes' writing: compassion. Although it is never explicitly stated, one feels that the author himself is touched by the deformity that life has produced in this man and compassion, of course, is the ultimate in character presentation; it is a trait that one finds in great novelists from Cervantes to Galdós. Compassion is achieved when the character takes over, in that transmutation whereby he becomes a living being, by which a character seems truly to have more life than even its author, a transformation that fascinated Unamuno. By his ability to achieve this, it is evident that Fuentes has thoroughly mastered in this book the art of penetration in depth. We are moved, the reader is involved, especially a reader who has sufficient knowledge of the Mexican background to understand and appreciate what Fuentes has done here. For it is not only the portrait of a man, but also of an era, an aggregation of evidence that depicts an epoch, a congeries of events that are made real through this man's living in them.

Poore, in his review already cited, calls this a "contemporary avant-garde" novel and comments that Eros has replaced Karl Marx in the emphasis. To say that is to misunderstand what Fuentes is ultimately trying to do—to give a *total* picture of a man —and to do so he must at the same time give almost as total a picture of the man's time. The erotic does not replace the Marxian any more than Marx outweighs any other factor in the man's life. Only in that one element of Cruz's development—his relationship with the "gringo" businessmen, noted previously—does the Marxian orientation show. Of course one may say that the total picture is also a condemnation not only of a man but of the society that produced him, a condemnation based on Marx; but that is not the point of this book, anymore than Cruz's erotic experiences are. Neither element preponderates in emphasis in the picture of Cruz's life and death.

Of more importance in our estimate of Fuentes' work are the remarks of Keith Botsford, in his article previously cited. Botsford starts off by saying that the work is ". . . a very personal and very ambitious novel from a man whose natural means of expression is the novel."[17] So far, so good. But then he goes on to get all entangled between Fuentes the man and Fuentes the novelist, and feels it necessary to qualify his first statement by saying that Fuentes allows dogmatic ideology to spoil the "essential seriousness" of his undertaking, that this is not truly "experimental" writing but rather a "collage of incidents . . . both unrealized and irrelevant." More will be said about Botsford's theories in Chapter 10, but anyone who has read *The Death of Artemio Cruz* with attention, without too many preconceived ideas and *on the author's terms*, will find it difficult to accept Botsford's strictures with any patience. One wonders indeed why he is so angry with Fuentes. He says, still in the same article, that he is finding fault with Fuentes "as a friend" and then goes on to charge that the style is wrong because it is "unnatural" and that Fuentes is, in effect, a provincial who has only partly assimilated the meaning of "eclectic." To other, less "friendly," readers of this work it seems clear that Fuentes not only fully understands the meaning of "eclectic" but has done a rather good job of assimilating many elements into a style that is effective and worth the effort of understanding that it demands of the reader. The fact that Carlos Fuentes can be a rude, impatient man should really not be allowed to affect one's judgment of his writing. There is also something to be said for the insufficiency of translations—it is always wise to consult the work in its original language if one's competence in that language is adequate.

We have spoken of the influence of Joyce, Dos Passos, Faulkner: it is evident in this work even more than it was in the first novel analyzed. It is unnecessary to labor the point. Fuentes himself once said that the only influence he admits to is that of Zane Grey—he was tired of being called derivative. Everyone knows that Joyce was the first major writer in English to use the stylistic devices that are now labelled Joycean; that Dos Passos employed what he was pleased to call "newsreels" and "camera's eye" techniques in his writing—Fuentes uses "tape recordings" similarly for some of Artemio Cruz's recollections. All of this is partly what makes Botsford so angry—he feels that Fuentes is using these stylistic devices, or tricks, deliberately, in order to produce a dazzling best seller and not because he is truly interested in experimental writing. Hence the charge of insincerity. A difficult charge to prove (or to refute) since it implies an access to Fuentes' professional conscience that it is unlikely anyone has, including Mr. Botsford.

Considerable influence of Martín Luis Guzmán is also discernible, not in style certainly, but in matter and content. It is a matter of point of view, as was mentioned in Chapter 3—Fuentes is doing what Guzmán did, analyzing, through the life of his protagonist, the society and the men produced by the Revolution. And the pessimism we have noted in both Azuela and Guzmán is also quite evident in *Artemio Cruz*—society and its cast are as corrupt as they ever were, in Fuentes' opinion. As Fuentes himself has said, first comes his point of view, his vision of the world; he proceeds from this to the material, and then to the characters.[18] There is even a parallel that could be drawn between Axkaná, the observer and narrator in Guzmán's *La sombra del caudillo (The Leader's Shadow)* and the same role played by Ixca Cienfuegos in *Where the Air Is Clear*. And of course, the

difficulty in classifying the work of Guzmán is equally applicable to that of Fuentes. Their work is the result of myriad formative influences and is equally eclectic.

Finally, *Artemio Cruz* is the work by which Fuentes' reputation was made, and we see in it all the elements, skillfully handled,
which have made Fuentes indeed a major novelist. From this
point on it is hardly necessary to talk further of development;
we will talk rather of fulfillment and lack of it.

IV   *Aura*

The novelette, *Aura* (the actual text is less than fifty pages),
was published in 1962, just before the publication of *Artemio
Cruz,* and its small reception was promptly overshadowed by
the much greater *réclame* accorded to the more ambitious work.
And even though chronologically it precedes *Cruz,* it is better to
consider it after *Cruz* since it is a work completely dissimilar to
any of the three previous novels and harks back to the short
stories. It is not much more than a long story, in so far as form
is concerned—an expansion of the tale already discussed in *Los
días enmascarados,* called "Tlactocatzine, del jardín de Flandes."
But it is much more elaborate than its prototype could be in
the evocation of a mood of slow-moving nightmare, of participation in a macabre fantasy.

Here shadow and substance are deliberately interchangeable,
dream and reality are indistinguishable. In this sense there is
also a great deal of the mood evoked later in "La muñeca reina"
("The Doll Queen"), in the collection *Cantar de ciegos.* Just as
Artemio Cruz is an eclectic combination of the style of *Where the
Air Is Clear* with the depth-presentation of character developed
in *The Good Conscience,* a combination of manner and matter, so
here we have a combination of the matter of "Tlactocatzine . . ."
with the mood of "La muñeca reina." This process is quite in line
with Fuentes' husbanding of his ideas, the maximum utilization
of material, that most writers practice, not so much because they
are afraid that they will run out of ideas as that they are fascinated by a certain quality or a certain manner that seems to
have interjected itself into their creative process and they wish
to let it develop. We touch here on the creative process itself, a

very uncertain realm, and one which authors themselves often prefer not to analyze.

In the hands of a writer like Fuentes, we must ask just what fantasy means. For Juan José Arreola, a Mexican writer contemporary of Fuentes, fantasy is the out-of-focus reflection of reality, the sudden vision of a startling other world, coexistent with the so-called real world—the physicists' theory of anti-matter applied to the realm of art—having almost some of the leprechaun quality of James Stephens' *Crock of Gold*. For Fuentes, fantasy is a protest *against* reality and not, as is commonly thought, a flight from it.[19] The function of fantasy in Fuentes is also somewhat like the function of dreams—a process by which the subconscious seems to cleanse itself while we sleep. This is not to say that he employs fantasy subconsciously, but rather that he takes the seemingly strange associations, the seemingly unrelated juxtapositions, the unlikely correlations that his subconscious presents and weaves them consciously into a tale which then becomes rather like a dream itself, a sort of nightmare of incubus and succubus, in which the participant swims in slow motion, knowing it is a dream yet strangely unable to break the spell.

We must note also that in this novelette Fuentes employs the *tú*-technique, in which the inner personality of the narrator speaks directly to, and at the same time intimately involves, the reader, who automatically responds by identification with the familiar form of address. This is a more complete identification of reader with narrator, not just partial as it was in *Artemio Cruz*, in which *tú* was only one-third of the personality of the protagonist. The effect is deepened by the use of the future tense for what would ordinarily be a present or even a past situation. Richard M. Reeve, in his review of *Aura*, feels that this stylistic device (the use of *tú*—he does not comment on the use of the future for further deepening of the effect) is probably derivative from the *nouveau roman* techniques, especially that of Michel Butor.[20] It is a deliberate juggling with devices that will, the author hopes, produce or reproduce the dream-like quality which is the essence of the tale. This attempt is further indication of the experimental quality of Fuentes' writing, since he is obviously trying to handle the novel, both here and in *Artemio Cruz*, as an object in itself which can be manipulated, like mirrors, to reflect the particular aspect of reality that interests the writer at the moment.

To elaborate a little more on Fuentes' view of reality and fantasy: for him fantasy is the world of the second reality and consequently he feels that all valid literary expression, apart from the pigeonholes in which it may be classified, must equally be an expression of reality.[21] Hence it is also equally valid, logically, to regard the physical book itself as an instrument for the expression of the reality of its contents (and, in effect, this book is illustrated). We must accept without cavil what he says about his theory of fantasy since, as G. K. Chesterton points out, the images of imaginative men are indisputable, and there is no question but that Fuentes is a fantast, an artificer of visions and dreams. These fantasies may not be ours, may not even be attractive to some readers; on the other hand, they may offer others many psychologically familiar and even attractive themes—all this will depend on the extent to which we, the readers, possess that common sediment of culture upon which all Occidental literature is based. This sediment of culture must now include more than simply a popular understanding of Marx or Freud, and in many cases needs an acquaintance with neo-Freudianism and what certain Communists call "Revisionism," to say nothing of many other ideas that have complicated our century. So we must accept Fuentes' interpretation of reality and fantasy, in its application in his literary efforts; but his ideas or theories about the social aspect of the world—these need not be accepted without cavil since, as Chesterton also points out, the ideas of logical and dogmatic men are disputable. We need not dispute them here, of course, since such disputation must be left to each individual reader who, in the modern meaning of the word, must be also his own critic.

The narrative framework of *Aura* is easily outlined. Felipe Montero, a young man, poor, a graduate historian, is looking for work. In reading the advertisements, he comes upon an ad that seems to be tailor-made, *Parece dirigido a ti, a nadie más* ("it seems addressed to you, just to you") (p. 9).[22] The use of *tú* immediately establishes the atmosphere of fantasy, the reader is plunged into the dream-world at the very beginning, an atmosphere is created that is remarkably well sustained throughout the tale. The unreality of content, again, will be reenforced by the reality of presentation—the carefully contributed details (the cigarette ash falling into the teacup, "you" pick up "your" briefcase and leave a tip, etc.)—all helping to make acceptable the immediate establishment of familiarity, so essential to successful fantasy. The style, in the meantime, creates the dreamlike atmosphere, the feeling we get of swimming effortlessly through a medium, that flowing quality that some cinematographers achieve (Ingmar Bergman in many of his films or Resnais' *Last Year at Marienbad*, based on an original script of Robbe-Grillet himself).

This dream-like atmosphere is established, as noted, at the very beginning and takes on a deepening quality as the story progresses, until at the end it has assumed the dimensions of nightmare—we are caught, along with the hero, inextricably in a literal embrace of horror, the same embrace of Tlazol in "The Gods Speak" in the first book of short stories, the embrace of the mad old phantasm of the Empress Carolta in "Tlactocatzine . . ." —an embrace which would end, of course, in death if we did not awaken and dismiss the incubus in the light of reality. The question implanted by the skillful writer is, do we in effect awaken and can we dismiss the incubus even in what we are pleased to think of as reality? Felipe Montero, the young historian of the story, does not awaken, and the last words he hears are those of the white-haired witch, the aged Señora Consuelo, as she seems to float around him, promising to evoke with her embrace the other figure of the young witch Aura, with whom he originally fell in love.

Señora Consuelo is immensely old; she is the widow of a general of the emperor Maximilian and she needs a resident historian to prepare her husband's memoirs for publication. This, as we know from fairy tales, is just the pretext all witches need in order to obtain power over their victims—the consent of the victim, in this case not to admit the witch into the victim's chamber but, as in a mirror, fantasy reflecting the "reality" of accepted myth, to gain the victim's willing entrance into the witch's realm. The young historian eagerly enters the trap, since it has been baited by the presence of a lovely young niece. Once he has entered, the realistic details of presentation begin to fuse with the fantastical aspect of the new reality: the doorknocker in the shape of a dog's head suddenly looks more like a canine foetus and seems to smile (p. 11), the dampness of the mossy patio, the odor of rotten roots, the thick pervasive perfume (p. 12)—all contribute to lend "reality" to the outer story and at the same time reenforce the effect of fantasy as we penetrate into the new inner story. And the witch's familiar is not a cat but a rabbit, whose red eyes shine in the gloom of her chamber.

That night, in residence in his new quarters, Felipe Montero hears a frightful, plaintive mewling which he traces to a garden behind his chamber—but next day he is informed that there is no such garden (pp. 29-30). This is the first of the increasingly palpable effects of horror. The house itself is always in shadows ("they have built all around us, Señor Montero, trying to make me sell . . ." [p. 27]), so that the young man can only half see objects and the old widow and the cats (that did, then, produce the mewling in the non-existent garden?) and even Aura herself are sometimes almost a blur, heard rather than seen. In fact, Aura seems almost an automaton, in terror of the old woman and doing only what her aunt permits, her eyes at times seem empty, and in a dream sequence (is it a real dream this time?) the succubus, in the form of Aura, naked, seems to visit him in his room and in his bed, resting on top of him, burning his entire body with her kisses (p. 35). He does not see her, the night is starless, but the perfume of the garden seems to permeate the firm young flesh in his arms and before they separate, exhausted, she murmurs in his ear, "You are my husband" (p. 36). Is any of this real? The effect, at least, is quite real—he falls in love with the shadowy Aura, he finds it increasingly difficult to work at the memoirs. And now the identification of Aura and the old woman begins—in the memoirs he reads that she was fifteen when her "future" husband knew her.

The clue to the spell is in French in the last line of Chapter III: *Tu es si fière de ta beauté; que ne ferais-tu pas pour rester toujours jeune?* ("You are so proud of your beauty; what would you not do to remain always young?") (p. 39). Now we realize (if we did not before) the identity of Aura. Although Felipe does not yet understand—after all, he is the victim and might still escape—we, the readers who are active conspirators with the author, will not try to escape since, with a delicious shudder of participation, we wish the culmination to be reached. Aura ages with the "action"—a girl of fifteen "when her husband first knew her," she now seems a woman in her twenties, then forty. At their next meeting, in her bedroom this time ,she washes his feet in the presence of the great wooden crucifix above her bed (pp. 45-46); they dance a strange waltz and end in a Black Mass on the bed, desecrating the Host on the altar of Aura's body. This is now authentic witchcraft and its purpose is to seal the victim to the witch forever, even "though I age" (p. 47). And again Felipe falls asleep—or was he asleep all along? But he is now becoming uneasily aware that he is beginning to confuse the two women. They seem to duplicate each other in action, speech, and being, they dress in the same colors. He finally makes the inevitable, feeble attempt to escape, to persuade Aura to run away with him, to leave the old widow. Aura answers that the old widow "has more life than I" (p. 51), that it is necessary to die before one can be reborn, and that Filipe must have confidence in her. And they make a tryst for that night in the very bedchamber of the old woman.

Señora Consuelo announces that she is going out, she will not be at home all day. Aura has already discreetly informed Felipe of this unexpected intention of her aunt—which is why they can make a tryst in her very room. No reason for this is given; none is needed; reality, while still evident in presentation, is now fused with fantasy and the stage is set for the dénouement. Felipe has the opportunity to foresee his fate, however; in the afternoon he looks at the third folio of the General's memoirs in which he, the General, speaks of his wife's, Consuelo's, experiments with potions and philters, her dabbling with witchcraft. The General comments on the complete alienation—in the psychic sense (pp. 55-56)—of his wife, and at the end of the memoirs are the faded old pictures—Aura is the young wife. Felipe now realizes where he is being led, but his will is gone, he cannot even think of escaping, and the final dream-reality takes place in the future tense: he will enter the bedchamber, he will find Aura there, he will kiss her withered breasts and caress her snow-

white hair, and even see, by the strange light that somehow per-
meates the habitual gloom, the aged face, peeling like a dried-up
onion (the metaphor is Fuentes'), down to the underlayers, like
those of a prune; he will kiss the fleshless lips, the toothless gums,
the very skull of the death-demon herself. . .

Fuentes himself thinks very highly of this story, he considers
it one of his best, and indeed we can agree with him that he has
achieved to a remarkable degree the fusion he has sought between reality and fantasy. The story is quite credible and convincing once you grant the basic thesis—not that witchcraft can
exist, that is purely a superficial level of the tale—that reality and
fantasy are merely opposite faces of the same coin; that what
we think we see in a mirror is just as real as what we think of
as the object reflected. The general opinion of most of Fuentes'
readers is also that this is one of his most effective stories. Reeve,
quoted before, says that "Many critics still consider *Aura* to be
Fuentes' best work to date and this reviewer is of the opinion that
it deserves much more attention than it has hitherto received."[23]
In the light of this general agreement, it might be interesting to
examine the opinions of a pair of critics who disagree. Luis Harss
and Barbara Dohmann (previously cited in Capter 6) give it
only a paragraph in their essay on Fuentes and condemn it by
stating first that it is based on a "bit of literary inanity," and that
the failure of the story to "hold up" even as a ghost story is due
to "structural" defects. But they do not tell us what the structural defects are. Perhaps they mean "structural" when they
state that it turns into a "mere fairy tale without suspense or
illusion." And, second, they feel that "Even the writing seems
lax and tenuous. Everything works out too easily."[24] They seem
to misunderstand the nature of a "ghost story" or of a "fairy tale."
This is not a "constructed" story (in the sense that a detective
story is, for example), that it must have "structural" (built-in)
suspense or easily recognizable "illusion." The suspense is that
achieved by suspension, or immersion, of the reader in an atmosphere that is at once real and fantastical; the illusion is the mirror-
like effect achieved by combining reality of presentation with
unreality of intention and style. As for the writing being "lax
and tenuous," these are unkind adjectives to apply to a deliberate effect achieved through style: the effect of dream-like atmos-

phere obtained through the use of *tú* and the future tense—"diffuse" and "diaphanous" would be adjectives more accurately descriptive of what is an intentional recreation of a mood, an atmosphere, that can only be contrived through the use of a style that is deliberately rambling and through a use of words that is purposely imprecise. Fuentes' use of words and his theory of such use will be touched on in Chapter 10.

The reason, on the other hand, that Fuentes himself has a high opinion of this work is that the theme—the question of identity, and reality—is one of his chief concerns. The fact that in this story the reader himself is involved in the question of identity is a gauge of its success as a story. All in all, we can fairly accept this novelette as a most successful presentation of one of the psychological aspects of reality and a successful evocation of the poetic value of fantasy. The fact that it has absolutely no "social" content or orientation is a welcome change from that expressed in the first three novels.[25]

V Zona sagrada ("Sacred Zone")

The first two novels, *Where the Air Is Clear* and *The Good Conscience,* held out the promise of future work from a talented young writer capable of developing in two main directions; the third and fourth novels, *The Death of Artemio Cruz* and *Aura,* fulfilled that promise by a successful fusion of the two modes in a most satisfactory artistic synthesis. It is a great disappointment, therefore, to realize that the fifth novel, *Zona sagrada* (Sacred Zone, Home Base, Safety, Sanctuary—the title means all of these ideas) is no more than a competent potboiler. Fascinated by character as Fuentes is, in this book he permits himself the difficult assignment of analyzing a mother-son relationship. Not content with the intricacy inherent in such an analysis on even the simplest level, he complicates his task by selecting a famous movie actress as the mother. We find again the same elements of style and presentation that he has used successfully before, but there is no new dimension. As a matter of fact, by the very choice of a noted screen actress to play the part of the neurotic mother, Fuentes diminishes the stature of the work—we all know far too well that actresses are neurotic to begin with. As the work progresses, it becomes apparent that the author, too, realizes the diminishing quality of her overwhelming presence, because he gives the novel a change of direction and concentrates on the effect of this relationship on the son. He attempts to present a complex and disturbing filiation and succeeds only in giving us a confused and disturbed case history. He is trying to present a study in psychological incest and madness, and to the extent of the limits within which he has placed himself, he at times succeeds. But these limits—the artificial boundaries imposed by the fame and wealth of the mother on the development of the son—are too restrictive and in the end limit the reader's interest simply because these people are too special.

The same stylistic devices that we have met before, the same attempt to fuse reality and fantasy, all applied to a young man who finally ends in madness because he was not sane (the Spanish word, *sano,* conveys the meaning better, since it means "sane" in the sense of healthy, mentally as well as physically) to begin with. This work was published in March of 1967, and we need not go into more detail because it cannot by any means be called an important work. The question of *why* Fuentes wrote it would be interesting but is beyond the scope of this essay.[26]

VI Cambio de piel (A Change of Skin)

Fuentes' sixth novel was published both in Spanish and English in 1967. Originally scheduled for publication in Barcelona early in that year, it was finally published in Mexico City at the end of the year. The change of publishers is of interest in that the content and point of view expressed in the work prevented approval by the Spanish government censorship. On the first of March, 1967, according to news dispatches, this work was submitted as an entry in the annual contest for the *Biblioteca Breve* and won the prize known as the 'Seix Barral" (because it was awarded by the Barcelona editorial house of the same name).[27] This prize is of high literary prestige in the Spanish-speaking world (its cash value is 100,000 pesetas, about $1,500) and the book was scheduled for publication naturally by the editorial house that gave the prize. However, the Spanish censor would not grant "clearance" and Fuentes had to seek a Mexican publisher.[28]

On the narrative level, the novel deals with four people, Elizabeth and Javier, Franz and Isabel, who are travelling by car from Mexico City to Veracruz, followed closely by another car in which the narrator travels. An accident to their car obliges the four to stay overnight in Cholula, that ancient city (and cemetery) of the pre-Hispanic Mexican world, and during the stopover (the "action" is contained in twenty-four hours), the narrator tells the multiple, complex "truth" about the four lives he observes.

The execution of the work reveals that Fuentes again uses all those "tricks" of style that are now his hallmark: intermingling of time-periods, languages and tenses, disconnected dialogue, the use of *tú* to indicate subjective projection, long "Naturalistic" lists of names and things, the painfully analytical narrative. The whole thing is the apotheosis of intellectualism applied to the telling of a story that is interesting but that leaves us with a definite feeling of *déjà vu*, something already met. Javier and Isabel especially are the old stock characters that we met in *Where the Air Is Clear* under the names of Rodrigo Pola and Betina Régules.

But even with the recognizable elements from his previous work, Fuentes does add a new dimension here (to say nothing of the new "cosmopolitan" characters, Elizabeth, Franz, and, finally, the narrator). The fact that *A Change of Skin* is full of previous components is of importance only because now in this work Fuentes carries them forward, develops them, and brings them to maturity. The style, for example, is the same but greatly amplified; the fantasy is controlled and expanded to new dimensions—the whole performance is a fascinating indication of Fuentes' growth as a novelist. Fascinating because, in contrasting this work with *Zona Sagrada*, using the same components, fulfilled, this work lives while that one does not. How is this to be explained? A Marxian tenet holds that quantitative changes bring qualitative changes: *A Change of Skin* bears witness to the truth of this dictum as applied to art. Simply by developing his techniques to a fuller degree, Fuentes has achieved a new quality, a greater magnitude, in his work. The technical structure is immensely more complicated here than that in his previous work. He employs not only ordinary flashbacks, but, as one reviewer says, historical (or time-machine) retrospects, in order to present his conception of the intricate intermingling of the lives of the protagonists.[29] Fuentes feels, apparently, that the spatial and temporal limits of history itself must now be manipulated in order to offer a "mosaic of the past, present and future."[30] In an interview (quoted by Robert E. Mead) that Fuentes accorded to Emir Rodríguez Monegal, the author proposed in this work to view the typically agitated lives of four twentieth-century protagonists against intercalated episodes from previous centuries in the same place.[31]

Another reviewer, George R. McMurray, calls *A Change of Skin* "an existential novel of protest" and believes that, of Fuentes' work, this "is probably his most significant to date."[32] Fortunately, we need not be detained by consideration of the "existential" aspects of the work, since our interest is primarily literary not philosophical (the work raises many correlated questions also, theosophical, spiritistic, racist, etc., none of which can be discussed here). That the work is "significant," however, is beyond dispute, since we can now see quite clearly the directions Fuentes has chosen to go, at least for the present. The development of his stylistic technique is now joined to a corresponding development of his fantasy/reality themes, what we might call the "Aura-theme" in his work. But in making the quantitative changes alluded to, simply by widening the treatment, so to speak, or deepening it, both in style and point of view, he has carried his work to complete fulfillment of the early promise, perhaps even beyond, to the point of inundation. The style, by these quantitative changes, has at times become cumbersome and interferes with communication: the reader is asked now not only to participate but to decipher; the fantasy, by the same simple augmentation, has gone beyond fantasy to the edge of madness (as a matter of fact, the "narrator," an invention by the name of Freddie Lambert, does indeed end in the madhouse, where he continues to hold imaginary communications with the protagonist Elizabeth).

One does not know quite what to make of all this. Is Fuentes legitimately pursuing a goal in artistic development or is he, like a runaway train, using the dynamics of his mastery of style and fantasy to carry his work off the rails of comprehension? It may be said, obviously, that he is merely developing the "approach" to literature (and all art) that is currently being exploited by many contemporary novelists (and other artists). The work is dedicated to Julio Cortázar, the avant-garde Argentine novelist, whose work Fuentes is known to admire. In saying this, we are simply stating that he is a part of the contemporary current in the arts. It might equally be said that he is writing phantasmagorias that will make good motion pictures.[33] This is the sort of judgment that must be left to posterity; we must limit our estimate of the work to what it means to us. McMurray calls it a "virtuoso" performance—but all of Fuentes' work is a virtuoso performance; that is to say the same thing Mead said when he calls Fuentes' early work a "tour de force." All this simply means that Fuentes is a good writer, unique in his way.

One more word on the development of the fantasy themes. The fact that in *A Change of Skin* we find these themes of myth-reality-fantasy carried to an almost anthropological extreme need not surprise us—these themes have dominated Fuentes' creative process since he began writing, even as a child. The rich Mexican myths still preoccupy him but he has greatly widened his interpretation. Xipe Totec, for example, the Aztec fertility myth, in his actuation among men (he feeds mankind, and thus saves them, through a symbolic, cyclic skinning, a change of skin) can now be equated with the Lamb of God, and in this widening of his understanding of these myths, Fuentes now sees that they are all archetypal (in the Jungian sense more than in that of Sir James Frazer in *The Golden Bough*) and treats them as such. However the critic may see Fuentes' handling of these themes, as Existentialist or Objectivist, they add up, in Fuentes' treatment of literature, to "a masterful interpretation of man's restless search for identity," an investigation into ". . . the causes of the dissatisfaction, loneliness and alienation which typify modern man and characterize the novel's four protagonists."[34]

Where will Fuentes go from here? It is useless to discuss his plans as he outlines them because, like all creative artists, he changes his plans as often as his inner needs and concepts fluctuate, almost according to mood. Whatever he comes up with,

we can be sure that it will always be interesting reading, for he
will undoubtedly allow his own increasingly cosmopolitan perspective to influence his future work, and his interest in myth-
fantasy-reality will no doubt continue to be a main concern. He
seems to have decided, in turning his back on Mexico (he now
lives "permanently" in Europe), that Mexico is not capable of a
continuing development of its national consciousness at this
time, even though the Revolution was, as is generally admitted,
the actual awakening of the national consciousness. It is tempt-
ing to read into this rejection of Mexico by Fuentes a psychological rejection of the inescapable *mestizo* character of Mexico and
of the Mexicans. In turning his back on his own country as a
place to live and work, he would seem to be symbolically
turning his back on his own heritage which, for whatever reasons,
is no longer acceptable to him. He feels, it would seem, that he
can best develop as an autonomous and self-fulfilling individual
by ceasing to be a Mexican. Other expatriate artists have been
able to achieve this kind of self-fulfillment—it will be interesting
to see what Fuentes does.[35]

CHAPTER 9

The Other Writings

JUST as the themes of his novels blend reality and fantasy, fact and fancy, so we might say that the themes of Carlos Fuentes' articles also fluctuate between the real and the utopian, depending on whether he is writing about the literary or aesthetic world, or the ideological world. By and large, his writings about literature and other genres are sensible, understandable, persuasive even when hypothetical; but his analytical writings about the application of Marxist theory to world problems are polemical and tendentious and can be dismissed as little better than high-class pamphleteering. Being a writer *and* an intellectual (and we have seen in Chapter 6 all that both imply), he seems to be particularly lofty when it comes to polemical writing. The facile mind of an intellectual seems, in his case, easily to become confused between commitment to ideological positions and the conviction that they are the *only* positions tenable; and when such a mind is guiding the facile pen of a born writer (which Fuentes is), the temptation is to try to persuade everyone that the positions lead inevitably to the correct solutions to all problems. With this cautionary word, we may proceed to consider the formidable output that has provided Fuentes with bread and butter during his rebellious years.

I Fuentes as Journalist

Since most of his "other writing" is journalistic, however, we must also make a few preliminary considerations about the nature of journalism because Fuentes has been a journalist almost to a greater extent, if linear output is considered, than he has been a novelist. Writing "journalism" may be a danger for a literary artist not simply because its nature is ephemeral but because it imposes a style and viewpoint of its own which may be crippling to "good" writing. Cyril Connolly has said, for example, that "journalism is loose, intimate, simple and striking; literature formal and compact . . ." He goes on to point out that "a writer who takes up journalism abandons the slow tempo of literature for a faster one and the change will do him harm." Further, it is evident that ". . . what is intended to be read once can seldom be read more than once . . . [and] the flippancy of journalism will become a habit, the pleasure of being paid and, still more, praised on the spot will grow indispensable."[1] The danger will obviously be less to a writer who, in his more formal work, has a "journalistic style" to begin with: loose, intimate, simple, and striking. Except for the adjective "simple," such a style is not unsuitable to Fuentes; and "flippancy" is usually observable in both forms of output if it is observable in either. The dangers Connolly foresees are pinpointed more precisely by Stephen Spender who believes that even more dangerous than the combination of journalism with serious writing is "a certain tendency to promote personal attitudes and habits into a whole view of life . . ."[2] We will elaborate on this in a moment, after pointing out that writers may justifiably seek adequate recompense wherever their society provides it if they cannot make an adequate living with serious writing. It may be recalled that ever since there have been journals, writers have found it convenient to earn extra money from journalism and in many cases it seems to have done them no harm (Dickens as an editor, for example; Ring Lardner as a reporter). We may say, with Spender, that in the case of Fuentes, it is precisely that personalizing tendency with regard to temporal attitudes, that constitutes the greatest danger, but in Fuentes' case the danger seems to be to his journalistic endeavors rather than to his serious writing. The latter has not greatly suffered (some of the short stories are perhaps too "loose, intimate, simple, and striking"), but the former has. Whether the dangers of journalism, then, affect a writer in his more serious work seems to depend to a great extent on the writer—just as some children never catch measles, so some writers never catch journalese, even when exposed to it.

Sometimes journalism may even offer a writer—at least a modern writer—an advantage that, if he is on his guard, will do him no harm but on the contrary may do him much good. Any modern writer must not only have the leisure and the isolation necessary for thinking about what he is going to write, and perfecting it in the writing, but *what* he is going to write about, the content, is to a great extent dependent on his own fullest participation in the life of his own time. Journalism may serve to make it possible for a writer to blend his own special world with the teeming experiences of the life of the world around him, and in whatever aspect of that other world that may interest him most. In the case of Carlos Fuentes, those aspects were first political and then, lately, increasingly literary and aesthetic. So, the two types of writing need not be mutually dangerous if they are kept on different levels. Just as two planes may fly the same course so long as one is above or below the other, so journalism and serious writing may be jointly practiced by the same writer so long as he keeps them apart. As Brian Glanville says, "Creative writing . . . from a deeper level than journalism, [is] one on which the imagination is engaged, trying to . . . transmute its material . . ."[3]

But journalism needs little imagination and most editors would blue-pencil any attempt to transmute material. With a writer like Carlos Fuentes especially, we must recognize that his own separation of interests makes it possible for him to write on both levels, with whatever damage there is accruing apparently only to the less serious writing. All the better, since if the bread-and-butter writing, by its very nature, is not "serious" writing then it obviously does not matter too much whether we take it seriously or not, or if it is "good" writing or not. But, in that case, why bother with it at all? And, indeed, at this point we may conclude that we need bother with it only to the extent that it is, after all, part of the total personality of the writer and as such must have some effect on the more important evaluation of his serious writing. What damages his journalistic output is what makes his other writing more interesting—that personalizing of attitudes mentioned above. The important matter is the interplay between the superficial attitudes, the temporal viewpoints, and their effect on the deeper-level thinking that produces the serious writing. Sometimes the journalistic-level attitudes come through almost intact, as for example, in the opinions expressed by Federico Robles, the banker in *Where the Air Is Clear*, with regard to exploitation and who should do the governing; or some of the reactions shown by Artemio Cruz towards his *gringo* collaborators in circumventing the laws of the Constitution.

This sort of thing, it would seem, might lead to literary schizophrenia in a writer, and, as a matter of fact, Dr. Edmund Bergler does indeed feel that most writers, in their own particular type of neurosis, do definitely show schizophrenic symptoms. If not to schizophrenia, such constant activity, such overproduction, must lead to exhaustion, to a nervous need (compulsive?) to constantly express one's opinions, to be not only a "talking machine" but a writing machine as well, which in turn can only aggravate the duodenal ulcer and the chronic colic. No wonder Fuentes occasionally feels the need to flee—it is not Mexico that weighs him down, but the over-demanding program of activity and productivity that he imposes on himself when in Mexico that gets him down. He says he feels the mountains closing in. In Paris, Rome, they do not close in because he permits himself much more social leisure there—his opinion is not always being solicited there (after all, in Europe a *Mexican* writer is not likely to be so solicited for articles as, say, Simone Beauvoir), he does not have to accept commissions from friends who have become editors or from editors who have become friends, he does not have to sit night after night in cafés endlessly chain-smoking and endlessly supplying dicta on every conceivable subject; he can even listen for a change—a great luxury for a "talking machine."

For Fuentes, New York has become almost as bad as Mexico City. Not quite so much solicitation, perhaps, and the pay is better, but since not only the actions of our Latin neighbors but their opinions have become of concern to us, there is much earnest seeking out of the "Mexican" point of view, or the "Argentine" reaction on the part of our editors, especially those that run intellectual magazines, such as *The Alantic Monthly*, and even some not so intellectual such as *Life en Espanol*. Fuentes has written for both, he covered the P.E.N. congress or convention for *Life en Espanol* in June, 1966, and has discussed Mexico today in the other. He has written letters assailing inter-

vention to the *New York Times*; he still has a regular contract
for regular articles with *Siempre!;* he has even written a theatre
report on Mexico for *Playbill.* His constant production makes
him almost as protean as Peter Sellers in the cinema. Let us take
a look at a few selected articles just to see what sort of thing he
has to say and how he says it.

II *Specific Articles*

Take, for example, his article in *Playbill.* It is a succinct (five
pages) and excellent account of recent trends in the Mexican
avant-garde theatre (which, let it be stated, is avant-garde only
from a provincial point of view). He starts, inevitably, with the
Revolution but very quickly gets to his thesis which is that "The
situation of the Mexican artist . . . has become very similar to
that of artists everywhere: they either offer the middle class what
it expects or live as outcasts from (yet very much a part of) it."[4]
He correctly awards to Rodolfo Usigli the position of "Mexico's
first real dramatist . . . [whose] treatment of middle-class life
was ironic and uncompromising . . ." but goes on to complain
that the younger writers, "these Mexican Tennessee Williamses,"
offer "false problems coated in sugary sentimentality or, worse
still, scenes of naturalistic degradation only to tickle the audience's self-indulgence. . . ."[5] The whole article, however, is an
excellent bit of reporting on the recent trends in the theatre in
Mexico, the current situation (at the time of writing) and the
"seething irrationality" of the government's ambivalent attitude
toward the popular arts, subsidizing with one hand and setting
unrealistic price schedules with the other. There is a certain contradictory attitude of his own, too—he praises the producers of
la carpa ("the tent") presentations, and blames the middle
class for the death of many slightly risqué themes, but one wonders just what the Mexican "proletariat" would get out of a
translation of *Oh Dad, Poor Dad* . . . or even *Murder in the
Cathedral.* We do not carp at the social attitudes implicit in the
article, but are trying to point out that those attitudes do not
necessarily lead to a true evaluation of the theatre in Mexico
today. There are just as many levels of sophistication among
audiences as there are among writers and producers and it seems

almost as absurd to blame the government for small attendance
at *Waiting for Godot* as it would be to blame Ionesco for the
popularity of a bedroom farce. The point is that personalized attitudes do color the article and we must remember Fuentes' Marxist orientation in everything he writes as journalism. And this
particular article is not even meant to be polemical!

For a purely polemical article, for the curious, any of his political commentaries in *Política* prior to 1962 would do; for something more readily accessible to the reader of English, a letter
dated Mexico City, May 17, 1965, and appearing in the Letters
to the Editor page of the *New York Times* for May 29, 1965,
will do. He is protesting the American intervention in the Dominican Republic and presumes to speak for all his fellows, since
he starts it off with "We, the independent intellectuals of Latin
America . . ." and adduces their independence by pointing out
that they also protested against the Soviet invasion of Hungary.
He defends revolution, as a Mexican who knows "only too well"
that a revolution passes through many contradictory phases, and
he goes on to make the statement—most difficult to defend, hence
not defended—that "Revolutions can take care of themselves if
left unharassed." Historically, this statement is completely inde-
fensible, but its sophistry is typical of polemical writing. Why
then all the screaming about "betrayal" of the Revolution—obviously it depends on who does the "harassing" and to what
ends. The usual emotional statements are made also: " We have
reverted to the law of the jungle in inter-American relations
. . ." and similar highly-colored attacks are made on the American President and the "antisocial, military regimes" that his pro-
tection sponsors. No validity is allowed to *raisons d'état*. Unfortunately, this is a typical, tendentious commentary which it is
hardly worthwhile reading, much less refuting. Some of his
articles in *Política* are a little better, since they are longer, more
analytical, less emotional, and show some evidence of an attempt at reasoning, if only along strictly Party lines. We have
all sampled these dreary, didactic "analyses" by various Marxist
theoreticians—nothing could be more boring; one wonders how
Fuentes could force himself to write them. In his case, it may be
supposed, often indignation accomplished what reason could
not.

There are literally scores, possibly hundreds of articles of varying topicality, interest, and levels of journalistic writing. A few hours spent browsing in the files and stacks of the *Hemeroteca Nacional* in Mexico City[6] reveals, for the last six months of 1962, just from *Siempre!*, the following topics written on by this prolific ideologist; "Xochicalco, altar de la muerte" ("Xochicalco, Altar of Death"), No. 472, July 11; "¿Qué, hará López Mateos con su fuerza?" ("What Will López Mateos Do With His Influence?"), No. 475, Aug. 1; "Doctrina Estrada para Perú" ("Estrada Doctrine for Peru"), No. 476, Aug. 8; "El frente de Cupatitzio" ("The Cupatitzio Front"), No. 479, August 29; "De Cupatitzio a Bucareli, con escala en Washington" ("From Cupatitzio to Bucareli, With a Stop in Washington"), No. 483, Sept. 26; "Atajemos la provocación" ("Let's Cut Short the Provocation"), No. 484, Oct. 3; "Agresión en América y paz en Asia" ("Aggression in American and Peace in Asia"), No. 486, Oct. 17; "Los motivos de Kruschev y la razón de Cuba" ("Kruschev's Motives and the Story of Cuba"), No. 491, Nov. 21; and so on. As is evident from the titles, most of these articles deal with topical political questions from a Marxist point of view (the subtitle of the Kruschev article, for example, is "Socialism Without Tyranny"). This was in 1962. By 1966 his interest has veered sharply (after the break with *Política*) from political questions to literary and related aesthetic matters. Still in *Siempre!*, No. 678 for June 22, 1966, for example, he writes on "Luis Buñuel y la libertad insuficiente" ("Luis Buñuel and Not Enough Liberty"). Let us examine this one more closely.

This article was inspired by the revival by the Cinématèque Française of Buñuel's Surrealist "masterpiece," *The Age of Gold* (Palais de Chaillot, April, 1966), but the title really serves as a springboard for that inevitable personalizing of attitudes which is Fuentes' (and, probably, that of all novelists turned essayists). His thesis seems to be that Buñuel is at last finding his real public: Youth. The young people are, according to Fuentes, revitalizing the great insights of Surrealism; games united to ethics are revolutionary (this seems a *non sequitur* at the very least); and audience and artist, hand in hand, today, through art, have taken on all the responsibilities of true liberty. A *roman nouveau* idea extended to all art. But this is merely the opening for his own ideas. He goes on to define liberty: to him it is the freedom of dissent, and can be found only in the relationship artist-spectator, and in the inviolable inner recesses where love dwells. From this he goes on to state that the triumph of modern technocracy means the disappearance of a traditional revolutionary outlook and of traditional democratic processes, the first having been submerged in the consumer society and the second by "the consecratory consensus of efficiency." The problem, as he sees it, is one of meaning, since two distinct ways of expression are face to face: the reductive language of bureaucracy vs. the universal language of artist-public; one derivative, the other constitutive; one impregnable, the other penetrable; one of answers, the other of questions; one for self-justification, the other for judgments; one for isolating, the other for communicating; one for the power élite, the other for men who are in the affluent society but not really of it. This is a lot of burden for two languages to bear. But taken all in all, the article is a commentary on the importance of art and its role in revolutionary and rebellious dissent, especially against the conformism of the other elements of modern society. Art must fight for all those aspirations (liberty, revolution) that Power (anonymous and absolute) condemns. It must, by its very nature, be heretical and unrealizable, and the only loyalty it need have is to itself, since realization would be the same as failure. At times Fuentes seems to get carried away by his topic. His own language in this article, for example, seems at times almost surrealistic itself. Is this possibly our old eclectic mimetism that was defined back in Chapter 4 as one of the *mestizo* characteristics of Mexicans? This is precisely the sort of writing, facile, persuasive, that Botsford condemns in his article previously mentioned as "insincere writing," the product of an experimentation with forms (or ideas) that have been only partly assimilated.

Fuentes certainly has a great deal of linguistic energy, there is no doubt about that—it is one of the characteristics of his writing that contributes to his persuasiveness. The reader is often carried along by the rush of his thought and the facility, even happiness of expression and phrase, that is one of his talents. Inevitably, however, on careful analysis there does seem to be some confusion of thought—a Surrealist quality in his very thinking that at times makes it most difficult to grasp, nail down, what he is actually saying, an elusive quality that is all very well in a novel like *Aura* (where it legitimately contributes to the atmosphere of reality-fantasy) but not so acceptable in a topical article.

In another article, on the contemporary novelist García Márquez (*Siempre!*, No. 679, June 29, 1966), he takes the opportunity to define beauty and humor, and, more importantly for our consideration of his work, myth. He distinguishes among myth, epic, and utopia, all of which, according to him, are reflected in, and have had great importance on, the history of Latin America. He says that utopia is pure projection, epic pure remembrance, but that myth unites nostalgia for the past to desire for the permanent present, and that all myth is external and communicable. This is more or less in line with the basic theme of his novel, *A Change of Skin*, and here we see precisely at work that effect that was mentioned previously—his journalistic idea being the surface presentation of an inner idea, of much deeper level, that will be of definite inspirational value in a serious work. This idea of deeper level is intimately tied up with his neo-Jungian, surrealistic view of reality/fantasy, which at present he is attempting to express through some of the techniques of the *nouveau roman*. And in his articles he does not lose the opportunity to turn a good phrase or two: *La Naturaleza tiene dominios. Los hombres, demonios* ("Nature has domains. Man, demons").

This preoccupation with a neo-Jungian concept of the collective subconscious, which Fuentes expresses through his own idea of Surrealism, is almost hilariously evident in an article he did on himself, again for *Siempre!* (a veritable showcase of his journalistic work!), No. 189, Sept. 29, 1965. This article is lavishly illustrated with completely inappropriate snapshots, obviously from his own collection, scattered singly and in collage throughout the article. The article itself is almost completely impish in its madness and of very little value, except indirectly, as a guide to what Fuentes is as a writer. He himself calls it a "literary striptease" but, we must hasten to add, one that leaves the stripper completely unrevealed. In this pose he is being, one suspects, "the Mexican Norman Mailer," the *enfant terrible*, still trying to shock the bourgeoisie. One wonders what *Siempre!'s* two hundred thousand readers made of it. The article does give some information on the genesis and writing of *A Change of Skin* (originally titled *El sueño* (*The Dream*), and he again underlines his now thematical idea that Mexico is to be understood only through its myths. Unfortunately, he seems to feel the need to enlarge this idea to the dimensions of an ideology (to replace, perhaps, the one he no longer believes in), and the whole thing becomes altogether too psychoanalytical, surrealistic, hermetic—impossible to follow. Such a view of Mexico is really too untenable and self-defeating and if he insists on pursuing his idea to its logical consequences, we will find his novels peopled by hieratic figures, portentously symbolic and nightmarishly oppressive. Some of this quality may be caught already in the characters of Ixca Cienfuegos and Teódula Moctezuma in *Where the Air is Clear* and if he is going to insist on this vision or amplify it, his work will become overburdened with incomprehensible telluric symbolism which most other Mexican writers have out-grown. There is a great deal more in this article—his ideas on government, art, revolutionaries, orphans, poets, novelists, what-have-you. It is indeed an exercise in logorrhea, a one-man flood, that leaves us gasping, shaken, and yet at the same time irritated because of the lack of mental discipline it reveals.

The Surrealist idea and his interest in it is validly explored, however, in an article he did on Leonora Carrington, the artist, scene designer, "the solitary witch and enchantress," as he calls her.[7] It is really an introduction to an article Miss Carrington presents, illustrated, of her life work. Interestingly enough, although she is a Surrealist, her prose is quite lucid. They met in their mutual work for the Mexican cinema industry. Such work, on scripts and various avant-garde films, has been a source of good income to Fuentes. According to Harss and Dohmann,

He has collaborated with Abby Mann on a film version of **The Children of Sánchez,** and worked with Luis Buñuel oin a cinematic adaptation of Carpentier's novelette, **El Acoso.** Recently . . . he has been active in experimental cinema . . . in rebellion against the notorious commercial tyranny of the Producers' Syndicate. He has contributed scripts, a couple of them derived from his own stories. They have helped spread his reputation both at home and abroad.[8]

Multiple interests, held together by an increasingly unified point of view, are the clue to this protean writer. He is still developing, still working his way through his own hinterland toward the inner core where he must expect to find his own true self. How many false idols are strewn along the way, how many attitudes, poses, posturings even, once thought to be valid, now discarded, litter the sides of the road! He turns his sights on his fellow writers in his article on the P.E.N. Club convention and declares that the Cold War is buried and that literary men are cannibalistic, each persuaded, way down deep, that he alone is right, his fellow writers fools, and the world indeed a stage on which each struts, mouthing his own version of the Gospel, hiding his own hollowness with the *personna*-mask, the image that he fondly holds, to deceive himself even more than his fellowman.[9]

CHAPTER 10

Appraisal

LET us begin by making good the offer of Chapter 7, to state, as far as is necessary in this essay, what considerations may serve as guidelines in the evaluation of Fuentes' work. Many literary historians feel that critical evaluation is not only unnecessary but actually impossible.[1] Without getting involved in intramural disputes, it may suffice, as a basis, to remind ourselves that the mere existence of norms at all implies some sort of philosophy, just as any exercise of discrimination or application of judgment must also imply criteria based in turn on the same philosophy. Inevitably, "The more complex a work of art, the more diverse the structure of values it embodies, and hence the more difficult its interpretation, the greater the danger of ignoring one or the other aspect."[2] Luckily it is not necessary here to enter too deeply into all this statement implies and it will be noted that eclecticism is as valuable in appraisal as it has been for Fuentes in the writing of his works. Indeed, it would be unprofitable not to be eclectic since each type of criticism available offers the possibility of seeing a work of art from a valuable point of view. The work itself, of course, must always be the center of attention and, in Fuentes' case, it must be kept constantly in mind even when the correlated aspects of his psychology or his sociology are discussed.

I *Unity and Selection in Fuentes' Work*

An attempt at appraisal implies the existence of some sort of "unity" in the body of work being appraised and therefore the first consideration is that Fuentes has aligned himself with the Objectivists. We have seen what this means and must point out the basic fallacy in their position; their rejection of the old auctorial omniscience, of the author as "central intelligence"—as long as there *is* an author, that Jamesian concept cannot be rejected, otherwise the Objectivists will be driven to resort to computerwriting if they insist on trying to maintain the logic of their theory (and even then, there will always be the Programmer). Enrique Laguerre, as was pointed out in Chapter 5, has already answered them.

With this basic statement on the Objectivists out of the way, we are free to go on. Fuentes' work invites the application also of such norms as those embodied in the following concepts: ". . . Experience is an evaluation of nature, in so far as it selects, modifies, arranges and orders nature . . ." and this experience is achieved via perception (first physical and then psychological), and ". . . literature, in turn, is an evaluation of the experience by individuals who are artists by virtue of their ability to put their evaluations into order through the imitative process involving the use of the symbols . . . we call words."[3] Selection is perhaps the most important evaluative device Fuentes employs, but account must also be taken of the inevitable distortion resulting from his selection, whether it be for a deliberate artistic purpose or simply as a by-product of his process of selection. Along with other factors in his process of selection, we must consider the non-rational in Fuentes' work, since he, like many contemporary writers, makes purposeful use of this element in experience. And in all these approaches to his work, the thread of unity must guide the reader since it, his work, is the product of a man who is theoretically and legally sane and must therefore have some sort of unified personality that is acting as the central intelligence.

As observed in his work, what is Fuentes' concept of selection? First of all, his selection of detail is based on his philosophy, then follow his choice of language, of arrangement, of emphasis, of final effect, keeping in mind that no matter how Objectivist a writer Fuentes may or may not persuade himself into thinking he is, his work is not simply documentary. From a consideration of his selective process (based on his life-philosophy) to a consideration of his techniques is the next step—Fuentes' use of allusions and their echo-value, the decorum or incongruity (purposeful or not) of his language, his use of figures of speech such as metaphor, personification, symbols, paradox, irony, etc., his use of parallelism and antithesis, of ambiguity, of outright mystification—all of these are important in each of his works which present "progression" in the unique world created by the writer.

Finally, in addition to the warning implicit in the occasionally observed fallacy of intention in Fuentes' work, a reader, before passing any sort of judgment, ought to read a Fuentes novel twice—once merely receptively and then (if it is worth it) in the same spirit in which the author wrote it. Basically, it does not matter what the book is *about*—it matters rather what the book *is*, and we must try to allow the book, as we would allow any work of art, to impinge upon us, to affect us, and "the first demand any work of any art makes on us is surrender."[4] A reader cannot tell whether it was worth receiving in the first place until he has received it in the first place. Does Fuentes' work meet what might be called the ultimate criteria—does it produce delight, recognition of its artistry, the successful combination of two distinct kinds of order by the author (the order of perception, physical and psychological, which he himself experienced; plus the order of presentation, the thing made, which he himself produced)? It is well to keep in mind what C. S. Lewis, the English critic, says, that "the truth is not that we need the critics in order to enjoy the authors, but that we need the authors in order to enjoy the critics."[5]

Beginning with the concept of selection, then, it must be clear that Fuentes, like other artists, bases his selectivity on his particular vision or interpretation of the world, of reality. He himself has said, as has been mentioned, that first comes his point of view, a vision that is ample enough to include an awareness of as many horizons as possible, even if his awareness is colored by his ideological position. Once adopted, this world view then becomes the rock beneath his feet, the wall at his back, the *point d'appui* from which he reaches out to sample the world and his selection of material and detail. Out of these multiple selections, his story and his characters grow. So Fuentes starts with viewpoint, proceeds to matter, then to material, and finally to character delineation and contributory detail, which go hand in hand. He takes these steps—since in any sort of organized writing it is inevitable that they should be taken—generally in the order outlined above, and then proceeds to the last step of all: the actual writing, which can almost be (or seem to be) automatic.[6]

II *Fuentes' Use of Language*

With these considerations stated, let us go on to the specifics in Fuentes' work. His use of language, for example, is one of the most important and revealing aspects of his art. His awareness, first, and finally his preoccupation with language began with his own bilingual development. A sudden insight in his childhood led him to the realization that many of the misunderstandings of peoples of different tongues rest on the inherent difficulty of adequately translating not words but ideas from one culture into another. He saw that this is much more than the simple semantic difficulty of choosing the *mot juste* in either tongue. To Fuentes, translation of ideas means understanding the actual historical, cultural and social context that led to the formulation of the idea in the first place, and then to its pithy statement in its native language in the second. "Manifest Destiny," "Monroe Doctrine," are phrases that mean totally different ideas to a Spanish American and a North American. Woodrow Wilson's intervention in Mexico (to "help" Carranza) was completely misunderstood and consequently unacceptable to the Mexicans and to Carranza in word and deed. This is a serious enough matter in any world situation, and is even more serious when the misunderstanding is between neighbors. So Fuentes, interested in understanding and being understood, from his childhood days in Washington broadened his concern with language in general until it became a concern with language as a subtle instrument, *his* instrument, for expression of meanings on all levels. And from there it is a step to an interest in language as a thing in itself, as an objective, concrete entity and not simply as a system of communication.

Fuentes felt that English as a language is much more vigorous, supple, and flexible than Spanish; that Spanish, less flexible and supple, is more stately and hence more formal. Sometimes he writes directly in English and sometimes his Spanish sounds "Englishy" to a purist. He himself has said that this is deliberate (it may also be partly a rationalization—a *post hoc* defense against the unkind critic who thought that *Where the Air is Clear* had originally been written in English), that he is trying to modernize (not anglicize) Spanish and even, at one time, make a Mexican Spanish. He acknowledges the influence of Salvador Novo, the contemporary Mexican poet, in his attempt to influence the style of the Spanish used in Mexico (and even, for that matter, in the rest of Spanish America and in Spain itself). In this endeavor he is not alone, nor is his preoccupation with the effect of language on style a phenomenon that is confined to his own approach to expression. Hemingway's style was influenced by his admiration for Spanish culture and especially for Pío Baroja, the great Spanish writer. The famous Hemingway style is to a large extent simply a transference to English of the Baroja style—typically the dry, short, declarative sentences. Tom Lea also, the author of *The Brave Bulls,* a Texan who also knew Spanish bilingually, writes a very "Spanishy" English, translating deliberately and literally from Spanish to English.[7] This is a stylistic device in all three writers, and Fuentes, in adapting English "suppleness" to Spanish, is again simply being eclectic. The critics who prefer to take a malicious "dig" at the process are either defending a purity of language that is a lost cause or may not be aware of what Fuentes is doing. Fuentes recognizes as do most contemporary writers that in the modern world languages will affect each other far beyond previously permissible points.

An equally important aspect of Fuentes' concern with language is his use of "forbidden" words—the short, four-letter words that in some countries are still forbidden because they are still considered obscene. Again, this is a deliberate device on his part, partly stylistic but chiefly didactic—his desire to "awaken" the masses, to get them to throw off the bourgeois hypocrisies that suffocate them. *Artemio Cruz* was considered "shocking" because it devotes several pages to an exploration of the word *chingar* in all its uses and phrases. But this is a slightly pedantic insertion in the work on the part of Fuentes—really a digression, since Artemio Cruz, as a man, was not particularly concerned with language as such—and is an intrusion, a semantic exercise, due to his ideological didacticism. He says that these forbidden words are sacred to him "as a defense, a defeat . . ."[8] Which is a way of saying that their use is part and parcel of his world-vision

and his concern with individual liberty. This is also his defense
of his so-called experimental work. In order to make this clearer,
it would be well to restate the matter, since we have now
reached the heart of the appraisal.

III   The *"Dual"* Aspect of Fuentes' Style

To date, Fuentes shows in his work two definitely discernible
currents, or trends: (1) that exemplified by his "social" novels
(*Where the Air Is Clear, The Good Conscience, The Death of
Artemio Cruz*)—stating his concern with individual liberty in
both a social and artistic sense; and (2) that exemplified by the
reality/fantasy theme, the fusion of these two aspects of man's
consciousness (*Aura, A Change of Skin*, many of the short stories,
and, to a certain extent, *Zona sagrada*). These two currents,
quite dissimilar, one an "outer," social concern, the other an
"inner," psychic concern, are the distinguishing characteristics
of Fuentes' work. It is possible to say that in his latest novel, *A
Change of Skin*, he has actually achieved a fusion of the two
trends, the social import with the fantasy treatment (Franz, the
ex-Nazi, Elizabeth, the American Jewess, caught up in a myth/
fantasy nightmare due to their association with the two Mexicans, Javier and Isabel). Since Fuentes' work, as is that of most
writers, is a projection of himself, this fusion of literary currents
might be considered symbolic of his own inner resolution of two
personality trends. But we do not wish to become too psychoanalytical in our appraisal, so we will leave this possibility to
other critics of Fuentes. It is evident that all creative artists are
complicated personalities and not until we reach, as far as possible for an outsider, some understanding of the basic conflicts
in the man can we even begin to understand his projection of
them in his work.

There is a parenthetical consideration in connection with his
attitude towards words and their use that is of interest to our
overall estimate of Fuentes. He says that his approach to words
is that of Humpty-Dumpty (whose use of words, it will be recalled, was quite arbitrary) and that his intention is to jolt Spanish and its speakers out of their *anquilosis* (he feels that Spanish
is ankylotic or, more popularly, arthritic).[9] This condition, in

Fuentes' opinion, is brought on by the "feudal" systems of thought still entrenched in the Spanish language—a historical condition, of course, which is now vestigial but nevertheless stultifying. How easy it is for Fuentes to go from the specific to the general, from ankylotic language to feudal systems of thought and thence to social systems to Marxism to experimental writing to Objectivism, etc. The man is all of a piece, and we can now begin to understand why he acts as he does and why he writes as he does.

Now, in turning our attention again to Fuentes' style, we may note that just as there are two basic concerns in his writing so there are two styles—one "experimental" and the other more straightforward (or Galdosian). This is an extension of an idea of Salvador Novo's—that one needs several styles to deal adequately with the modern world—an idea that Fuentes has channeled into the dual development so acceptable to his personality. As we have noted, Fuentes has fused the two currents, previously described, in his latest work; similarly, he has also fused the two styles. Perhaps it would be better to say that the narrative style has been swallowed up by the experimental style, since he seems to have definitely decided that this is his preference. Speaking of styles, this may be seen as the triumph of the "inner" reality over the "outer"; and similarly, in his two currents, the myth/fantasy reality is rapidly superseding the "social" reality in his interest.

Besides the larger areas of language and thematic direction, Fuentes' style should also be discussed from the point of view of arrangement, emphasis, use of allusions, figures of speech, etc., all elements previously listed at the beginning of this chapter. We will not do so, however, for two reasons, (1) Fuentes is too much an experimental writer *and* an experimental thinker to be pigeonholed yet on these considerations—to date he is only forty-two, and may discard tomorrow all that he has done so far, and (2) in the final analysis, such classification is too much a matter of an individual critic's personal preferences and would therefore be invidious in an essay about a still-living contemporary writer. To a certain extent the New Critics are right—the reader must go to the work itself and determine for himself whether he agrees with or rejects the author's point of view, whether he finds pleasing or displeasing his use of language, whether, finally, he is a "good" writer *for him* or not. This is ultimately the only way to judge a work and all the technical considerations of pedants will not alter the final acceptance or rejection of that work by the reading public as such even though they may, at the moment, influence some of the buying public. Fuentes, in his works, invents a fictitious but believable set (in the theatrical sense) for the presentation of a "real" or "fantastical" action (in the literary sense) and whether we, the readers, are entertained and convinced or even touched by his presentation depends almost as much on what we bring to the reading as on what he puts into the writing. To that extent, then, the theory of the *nouveaux romanciers* is correct—the success of a work of art does depend on the collaboration of writer-reader, just as, in other fields, it does on artist-viewer, musician-hearer.

IV *Final Considerations*

There are a few points mentioned in previous chapters remaining to be cleared up. We have pointed out the influence of Azuela on Fuentes, the "diagnostic" point of view, which has already been discussed. But there is one notable difference: Azuela in all his work defends (implicity, not explicitly) the inherent dignity of man, especially of the "little" people, even when they are caught up in the complexities of the urban jungle (the "neon wilderness" of the *tremendistas* and the city novelists); Fuentes sees no dignity in the human spirit, it is a cringing opportunist, the inner "ape," the primitive caveman, fighting for survival. Aside from the odd fact that Fuentes, the Marxist, should reveal this attitude, the difference is apparently a matter of generations—Azuela still retained some vestiges of the old philosophical concepts of liberal democracy, Fuentes was influenced by the neo-Freudian, behavioristic ideas of contemporary synthesists. The influence of Martín Luis Guzmán on Fuentes has been chiefly intellectual. Both are much more so in their approach to social and novelistic problems than was Azuela. It is the same sort of difference one notes in the work of Diego Rivera and José Clemente Orozco: the latter is much more visceral, the former much more didactic. Rivera is the Guz-

mán of art (or, if one prefers, Guzmán is the Rivera of the novel),
Orozco is the Azuela of art (indeed, some of his engravings might
well serve as illustrations for *The Underdogs*). In the case of
José Rubén Romero, it is his and Fuentes' mutual concern over
social injustice that is the point of influence, although Romero
would cure it with laughter whereas Fuentes would (or would
have, since he is growing away from ideological nostrums) cure
it with Marxism. Parenthetically, it is to be hoped that, as
Fuentes outgrows the need for authoritarian systems of thought,
he may develop more humor. Humor depends on inner relaxa-
tion, and Fuentes is not a relaxed man; despite the social poise,
there is a deep inner tension, betrayed by the chain-smoking. As
a matter of fact, Fuentes feels that humor is equal to compassion. But this is a messianic concept of humor, a "release" he
(the artist) offers to the poor sufferers from social injustice. Humor may well be compassionate, but it is much more, as Romero
has shown us in his work.

The influence of certain European and Anglo-American writers on Fuentes is so well known that we have preferred to trace
deliberately more fully the influence of certain key Mexican authors. It is inevitable that the latter, the Mexicans, must have
had a strong germinal influence on a man who for so long was so
concerned with what it meant to *be* Mexican and with what
Mexico was. Any writer living and working in Spanish in Mexico
during the last two decades must have been influenced importantly by these great predecessors.

We have mentioned, in passing, something of the social image
that Fuentes seems to enjoy projecting: the social or society pet,
the dilettante, the international playboy. There is an almost
childish delight in some of his participation in the activities of
what is today, lacking anything else, the *haut monde* of the Western World. To participate, he needs an adequate income and
to that extent his work (at least his journalistic and topical writing for the cinema, for example) is influenced by commercial
considerations. His background is such that he does not "worry"
about money, although the icing on the cake must be bought by
his own earnings. So, his personal liberty is inevitably circum-
scribed by the need to participate, a condition that is set by his
own appetites, and which, in turn, is limited by the market-

ability of what he produces (another reason to be wary of the journalistic production). There is no reason to condemn him for this "commercialism" since the days when writers starved in garrets are gone and any writer who makes his living by writing is automatically a "word-merchant," selling dreams for gold, but this does not necessarily make him a bad writer. Fuentes seems to have been quite successful in separating the two types of writing and, if anything, as stated, his serious writing affects his journalistic efforts rather than the other way around.

For the last time, we must refer briefly again to Botsford's charges of provincialism and "insincere" writing. The most serious charge is that of provincialism, which Botsford bases on the premise that provincial art is traditionless and that therefore basically *all* Latin-American art is provincial. Aside from the obvious snobbery of such a sweeping generalization, he reenforces this argument by stating that Fuentes' use of an experimental technique (in *Artemio Cruz*, specifically) is an attempt to take over a *foreign* tradition which he has only partly assimilated, and which is therefore "unnatural." He states finally, as a corollary, that a novel is a variety of experiences collected under a single view, and that this "unity" is what he does not see in *Artemio Cruz* and hence in Fuentes. The main difficulty here seems to stem from the use of the term "traditionless" in one sense and the use of the term "provincial" in another. Botsford seems to be using "provincial" in a geographic sense, and the two meanings are not compatible. "Unity"—within the wide meaning permitted by the eclectic framework, of course—is precisely what Fuentes has achieved. If Botsford is talking about *structural* unity (the fact, as noted, that some sections of the novel "speak" from Catalina's point of view, for example), he does not make this clear. Unity is, in fact, Fuentes' great achievement, in *Artemio Cruz* and elsewhere, one that he shares with other writers of his generation. A man is no longer a "Mexican" or an "Argentine" or a "Uruguayan" writer—one is a writer in the Western world, in the literature of the West, who happens to use English, or Spanish, or French, or any other of the European languages, for expression. To that extent, Fuentes and his generation have precisely achieved what the Revolution was all about —universality through nationality—and that is what was meant back at the beginning of this essay when we said that Fuentes should not be classified as a "Mexican" writer. He is not provincial precisely because he is no longer Mexican in the narrow geographical sense of the word even though his settings may be local. The fact that he is not provincial is also as much a matter of style as it is of world view, and both are as international in *Artemio Cruz* as they are in any of his works. Botsford has not seen the forest because of his concern with the trees, a danger critics run when they get bogged down in technical considerations of style or of thought.

A literary artist, it would seem, should primarily be concerned with recreating life according to his vision of it, and that is what Fuentes does. His vision of it is complicated and personal and influenced by many factors, the most important of which we have attempted to analyze. Fuentes' vision of life was first of all his vision of Mexico—the archetypal Mexico, the "myth" of Mexico, as Fuentes understood it, and that is why this essay is not only about Carlos Fuentes but also about his Mexico.

Notes and References

Chapter One

1. Paul Rogers, *Escritores contemporáneos de México* (Boston, 1949), p. xix.

2. In my observations on the *Ateneo*, here and in the rest of this chapter, I am indebted to Patrick Romanell, *Making of the Mexican Mind* (Lincoln, Nebraska, 1952) and to Samuel Ramos, *Historia de la filosofía en México* (Mexico, 1943). See also Note 11, below.

3. M. Alesio Robles, *Historia política de la Revolución* (Mexico, 1946), p. 9.

4. Father of the contemporarily famous Alfonso Reyes; he was sent by the wily old dictator to Europe, but returned after the fall of Díaz, to take an active part in politics, especially, in the uprising against Madero in February, 1913.

5. Government troops obeying, it is said, direct orders of Díaz himself, shot down more than 200 strikers in the Río Blanco area. The *científicos* (the "scientists") were a group of administrative advisers to Díaz, formed originally by his brother-in-law, Manuel Romero Rubio, organized to govern "scientifically"; however sincere they may have been at first, this group soon used the "scientific" label to cover up its own unscrupulous manipulations of economic legislation and of the stock market.

6. Charles G. Cumberland, *Mexican Revolution, Genesis under Madero* (Austin, Texas, 1952), pp. 27-28.

7. For the interested reader, an excellent one-volume history of Mexico, in English, is that of Henry Bamford Parkes, published by Houghton Mifflin Co., Boston. In the 1938 edition, see pp. 324-34 for the Madero chapter.

8. The classic on this period of the Revolution is, of course, Mariano Azuela's *Los de abajo*—several good translations are available in English, the latest, *The Underdogs*, being a study by Beatrice Berler, Trinity Univ., San Antonio, 1963.

9. Martín Luis Guzmán, for exomple, was an admirer of Pancho

Villa; Luis Cabrera preferred Carranza; Vasconcelos admired Obregón; López Portillo Rojas, originally a *maderista*, later sold out to Huerta, bribed by the Ministry of Relations portfolio in the usurper's cabinet; even the fiery old Modernist poet, Salvador Díaz Mirón, praised Huerta in verse, a mistake that sent him into exile later.

10. There is a definite pattern discernible in the work of the writers and artists who reacted to the Revolution: the older generation, such men as Azuela and Orozco, was generally pessimistic; later artists have become more optimistic—see specifically Jesús Silva Herzog's remarks in his *Ensayo sobre la revolución mexicana* (Mexico, 1946).

11. Justo Sierra, humanist, educator, historian, was Minister of Public Instruction in Díaz' cabinet. The *Ateneo de la Juventud (Atheneum of Youth)* was founded by Alfonso Reyes, Antonio Caso, José Vasconcelos, and their Dominican colleague, Pedro Henríquez Ureña—their views and ideas had considerable influence on the writers and artists of the period between 1910-1925 especially, although of course more diffused effects have been felt far beyond the last date.

12. See Romanell, *op. cit.*, pp. 146, 56-57 *et passim*.

13. From a letter of the Mexican historian and journalist, Octavio J. Guzmán ("Mateo Podan" of *La Prensa*), dated Sept. 26, 1956, to the writer.

14. Romanell, *op, cit.*, p. 63 (his italics).

15. See particularly such writers as Alfonso Taracena, *En el vértigo de la revolución mexicana* (Mexico, 1930), p. 229; and Francisco L. Urquizo, "*Recuerdo que . . .*" (Mexico, 1934), pp. 17, 28, 335-36.

16. This has been particularly true in the theatre: see for example, Juan Bustillo Oro's *San Miguel de las Espinas*, Mauricio Magdaleno's *Emiliano Zapata*, Francisco Monterde's *Oro negro*, among others.

Chapter Two

1. Oral because their hieroglyphics could only express facts for the most part and, by symbols, some subjective conditions—a stage of development that did not permit the communication by writing of effective poetry. Among the specific examples are of course the *Popol Vuh* of the Mayas and certain fragments of an epic or lyric

nature of the Nahuas, some of these attributed to Nezahualcoyotl, king of Texcoco in the fifteenth century.

2. Samuel Ramos, *Perfil del hombre y la cultura en México* (Mexico, 1938); see also his *Historia de la filosofía en México,* (Mexico, 1943).

3. M. Alessio Robles, *op. cit.,* pp. 375-76.

4. Miguel Mazin Cervantes, *La Revolución extraviada* (Mexico, 1935), pp. 204-44.

5. See Luis Cabrera's statistics and analysis in Ch. 2 of *Renascent Mexico,* edited by Herring & Weinstock (New York, 1935), pp. 11-29. According to the *Britannica* (14th ed., Vol. 15, 381), the *mestizo* population of Mexico was 21% in 1810, 40% in 1900, 61% in 1945. According to Cabrera, it was 70% in 1935. Since he was high in government circles and had access to all figures, I prefer to accept his data.

6. Ramos, *Perfil* . . . etc., cited above in Note 2, p. 208. Vossler says much the same thing in his essays on Spanish literature.

7. Cárdenas distributed more than twelve million hectares of land; the *Banco Ejidal* was reformed so that loans could be made more directly to the farmers and their cooperatives; the campaign (which Morrow had persuaded Calles to forget) for controlling the great foreign capitalists and their investments in Mexico was renewed; and the exploitation of the industrial workers by Luis Morones and the C. R. O. M. (*Confederación Regional Obrera Mexicana;* organized in 1918, it reached the height of its power in 1927 when it numbered over two million members, all under the absolute control of the repulsive Morones, who set up the *Grupo acción* to help perpetuate the power of Calles) was eliminated by the administration-supported creation of the *Confederación de Trabajadores Mexicanos* headed by Lombardo Toledano (who had been called "an honest Marxist"). Also the presidential term of office was constitutionally extended from four to six years.

Chapter Three

1. By "Romantic thesis" I mean here a certain attitude toward life, illuminated by sensitivity and imagination, that is generally expressed through individualism, rebelliousness, libertarianism; through mystery, fatalism, the picturesque, and the exotic.

2. There is no point in discussing the neo-Classicism of such

writers as Gorostiza and Pesado; or even other Romantic writers, such as Calderón and Castillo—the currents they swam with were for the most part outside the stream of truly Mexican literature—they were not Mexican writers but neo-Europeans.

3. Azuela himself (in his *Cien años de novela mexicana*, Mexico, 1947) calls these writers "realists in spite of their defects"—the defects being the non-realistic elements in their works. It seems to me one might equally well call them realist *due* to their defects, since it was their very eclecticism that makes them all the more authentically Mexican.

4. *Hispanismo* (a cultivation of the hispanic elements in the Mexican character; the opposite of *indigenismo*) was championed later by Vasconcelos in one of his "phases"; *estridentismo* was one of the literary groups, especially in poetry, that flourished, chiefly as a reaction to Modernism, in the 1920's.

5. Manuel Pedro González. *Trayectoria de la novela en México* (Mexico, 1951), p. 103.

6. F. Rand Morton, *Los novelistas de la revolución mexicana* (Mexico, 1949), p. 185.

7. Although *Los de abajo (The Underdogs)* was not known to the general reading public until 1925, it was written in 1915.

8. Personal comments and impressions on Azuela and other writers here and in subsequent pages are based on many talks with my father, Ing. Octavio J. Guzmán, writer and journalist, a personal friend of Azuela and Orozco and well acquainted with practically all the other men of the Centenary Generation. Since 1928 he was associated with *La Prensa*, as columnist, managing editor and part owner, and was intimately a part of the cultural life of Mexico of his time (1881-1963). This has made available to me information about many of the men and events discussed that would be unobtainable elsewhere.

9. Arturo Torres-Rioseco, *Grandes novelistas de la América hispana: I. Los novelistas de la tierra* (Berkeley, Calif., 1941), p. 27.

10. Both quotes are from Enrique Anderson-Imbert, *Historia de la literatura hispano-americana*, lst. ed. (Mexico, 1954) p. 302 and p. 303.

Chapter Four

1. It may be objected here that certainly some of the works of Carlos Fuentes seem most pessimistic. At this moment, all I can

say is that it is not the same sort of pessimism (not so "Mexican," not so "national") as that of Azuela, it is more cynical and more personal—all of which will, I hope, be made clear in subsequent chapters. One is the pessimism of a vision of society, the other is that of an individual who is an observer of a scene that happens to be Mexican: he observes his characters and their actions as an individual, not as a Mexican. There is a subtle difference.

2. There is an amusing anecdote illustrating the extreme intransigence of one well-known *indigenista* who also happened to be a Communist. Diego Rivera claimed that he wished to restore the Aztec practice of human sacrifice and spoke highly of the mystical and poetical qualities of the rite, and his wife at this time, Lupe Marín, observed that she feared he was eyeing her as a possible victim.

3. It will be understood, I trust, that the word "Hispanism" here and later on is being used as an inclusive term (containing equally the idea of all those currents that flowed away from the native) and not in the more restricted sense in which Vasconcelos developed the idea into an aesthetic credo.

4. From "La suave patria" ("The Sweet Fatherland"), published in a posthumous collection under the title of *El son del corazón (The Sound of the Heart)*.

5. Among other works, Obregón Santacilia is the architect of the controversial Monument of the Revolution (popularly known as *La Gasolinera* [The Service Station]), although the building which most shows his successful adaptation of the integralist ideas is the imposing *Instituto del Seguro Social* (Social Security Institute) on the Paseo de la Reforma just below the Diana fountain. Silvestre Revueltas was a protégé of Carlos Chávez: his *indigenista*-nationalistic perspective is evident in such works as *Cuauhnáhuac* (1930), a musical picturization of Cuernavaca, and *Janitzio* (1933), inspired by the island and the great monument to Morelos that stands on it.

6. For those interested in a complete review of the term and its meaning, see Andrés Molina Enríquez' *La revolución agraria de México*, 4 vols. (Mexico, 1932), especially Vol. I.

7. These statistics are taken from the same source cited in Chapter 2, Note 5.

8. M. P. González, *op. cit.*, p. 14.

9. From a conversation with an intimate friend of Fuentes', who prefers to remain anonymous, in Oct., 1966.

10. The definition here given is a paraphrase or restatement of that to be found in Webster's New International Dictionary (1928 edition).

11. Quoted in *Time,* August 12, 1966, p. 49.

Chapter Five

1. Cf. Ramírez de Aguilar's critical essay, *"La decadencia de la novela en México,"* in *EXCELSIOR* for Monday, July 30, 1962, p. 10-A.

2. Blanche Gelfant, *The American City Novel* (Oklahoma, 1954).

3. See Robert Elliot Fitch's article, "Mystique de la Merde," in the *New Republic* for Sept. 3, 1956 (Vol. 135, No. 10).

4. See particularly his novel *¡Vámonos can Pancho Villa! (Let's Go With Pancho Villa!)* (Madrid, 1935), pp. 34 and 27.

5. See David Daiches' *A Study of Literature for Readers and Critics* (Ithaca, N. Y., 1948).

6. Janet Winecoff, "The Spanish Novel from Ortega to Castellet: Dehumanization of the Artist," *Hispania* (March, 1967), (Vol. I., No. 1), 35.

7. *Ibid.,* p. 39. I am greatly indebted to Dr. Winecoff for clarifying many of the points expressed in this chapter about Objectivists and the *novela nueva.*

8. See José María Castellet, *La hora del lector* (Barcelona, 1957), the first chapter of which is called *"Las técnicas de la literatura sin autor"* ("The Techniques of Authorless Literature"), quoted in Winecoff's article listed in Note 6, above, p. 42.

9. Enrique Laguerre, the contemporary Puerto Rican novelist. His observations, which I have translated and paraphrased, are from a lecture he gave at Queens College, Flushing, N. Y. on Wednesday, March 22, 1967.

10. Winecoff, *op. cit.,* p. 39.

Chapter Six

1. The basic facts on Fuentes' are taken from the following sources: the data sheet provided by the author's publishers, based on the Author's Questionnaire that forms part of their private file on the man; the *New York Times* Index and microfilm Reference Library; other published sources, i.e., essays by critics, newspaper

articles, etc.; and last (although generally most interesting), information supplied by close friends, relatives and acquaintances (most of whom prefer to remain anonymous). Fuentes himself is a poor source since he takes a mischievous delight in mystification for its own sake and enjoys misleading "pedants" by supplying erroneous data.

2. Robert G. Mead, Jr., recounts an interesting anecdote in connection with this period in Fuentes' life, in his article "Literature and Politics: Our Image and Our Policy in Latin America," *Hispania* (May, 1966), p. 305.

3. Fuentes was of course familiar with the work of Romanell and Ramos, cited in Chapters 1 and 2, as well as with the work of the founders of the Ateneo. The great and personal influence of Alfonso Reyes will be alluded to further in Chapter 8. For more background information, the interested reader will find an adequate bibliography in my own work, *México épico* (Mexico, 1962, pp. 269-76).

4. Quoted in Note 4 of the Robert G. Mead, Jr., article on "Carlos Fuentes, airado novelista mexicano," *Hispania* (May, 1967), p. 235.

5. See *El haz de leña (The Bundle of Firewood)* by the well-known Spanish dramatist, Núñez de Arce (1832-1903), for the effect of such a sensational declaration.

6. The columnist was Víctor Rico Galán, whose articles were of such snide sophistry that only the dedicated party-liner could read them with a straight face.

7. See the *New York Times* for April 7, 1962, p. 2, column 8.

8. See essay number 8, "Carlos Fuentes or the New Heresy," in *Into the Mainstream,* a collection of conversations with Latin-American writers, by Luis Harss and Barbara Dohmann, published in New York in 1967, pp. 276-309 (the quotation is on p. 282). I am much indebted to this essay for corroboration of some of the information I received from personal sources.

9. In addition to the work mentioned, see also Bergler's *The Revolt of the Middle-Aged Man.*

10. Harss & Dohmann, *op. cit.,* Note 8 above, p. 283.

Chapter Seven

1. *The New Yorker,* Jan. 7, 1967, p. 91.

2. We must keep in mind the difference between humanoid and subhuman, of course; the difference between, say, the characters of a Dostoevski and a William S. Burroughs.

3. Robert G. Mead, Jr., "Carlos Fuentes, Mexico's Angry Novelist," in *Books Abroad*, Autumn 1964, pp. 380-82.

4. *Ibid.*, p. 381.

5. Both quotes are from Bacon (Wallace A.) & Breen (Robt. S.), *Literature as Experience* (New York, 1959), p. 215.

6. From an article Fuentes wrote on the cinema in Mexico for *Siempre!*, No. 632, August 4, 1965, VII.

7. *Ibid.*

8. *Cantar de ciegos* (Mexico, 1966), 2nd ed., p. 83.

Chapter Eight

1. In "Un juego de espejos enfrentados," *Life en Español*, August 2, 1965, pp. 22-26.

2. Keith Botsford, "My Friend Fuentes," *Commentary*, February, 1965, pp. 64-67.

3. Farrar, Straus & Giroux, 19 Union Square West, New York, N. Y. Most publishers are reluctant to give exact sales figures.

4. The title of Emir Rodríguez Monegal's article, cited in Note 1, above.

5. Fuentes broke with Reyes sometime before the death of the latter in 1959. Precisely why is not known but some of Fuentes' friends think that the break was due to the differences in generation and in social outlook of the two men: Fuentes was a Marxist, Reyes had no more than an intellectual's interest in Marxist theories and resisted Fuentes' arguments and attempts to "convert" him.

6. All quotations are from Sam Hileman's translation of *La región más transparente* (New York, 1960).

7. See his interview with Emmanuel Carballo, reproduced in the latter's *Diecinueve protagonistas de la literatura mexicana del siglo XX* (Mexico, 1965), pp. 427-48.

8. Originally, *Las buenas conciencias* was to have been the first volume in a series to be titled *Los nuevos (The New Ones)*, and is so listed in some catalogues.

9. All quotations are from the edition (translator's name not given) of Ivan Obolensky, Inc., New York, 1961.

10. Throughout the interview cited above, Note 7.

11. As stated previously (Chapter 4, Footnote 9), much of the "personal" material given on Fuentes has been received from friends who prefer to remain annoymous.

12. All these quotes are from his Review, published on the book review page of the *New York Times* for Tuesday, May 19, 1964.

13. Quoted in *Excelsior*, Mexico, D. F., 26 August 1966.

14. Carballo, *op. cit.*, in Note 7 above, p. 440.

15. *Ibid.*, p. 430.

16. All quotations are from *La muerte de Artemio Cruz*, 2nd edition (Mexico, 1965)—my own translations; this quote is on p. 316.

17. See Note 2, above.

18. Carballo, *op. cit.*, p. 436.

19. Carballo, *Cuentistas mexicanos modernos* (Mexico, 1956), Prologue to Vol. I, xxxi.

20. Richard M. Reeve, *Hispania*, May 1966, p. 355.

21. Carballo, *op. cit.*, in Note 7 above, pp. 427 and 428.

22. All quotations are from the Era Alacena first edition (Mexico, 1962); my translations.

23. Reeve, *op. cit.*, p. 355.

24. Luis Harss & Barbara Dohmann, *Into the Mainstream* (New York, 1967); all quotations are from p. 302.

25. According to Fuentes' publishers, this tale was to be made into a motion picture, but there has been no further news on this project as of this writing (May, 1969).

26. There is general embarrassment over this work in Mexico amongst Fuentes' friends and critics. It is felt to be a transparent novelization of the life of the famous actress, María Félix, and her relationship with her son, and it is felt that Fuentes has shown singularly bad taste, to say nothing of betrayal of friendship, in writing it. This is perhaps slightly exaggerated since Miss Félix's real son is quite sane and healthy and earning a good living as a young television actor in Mexico City. However, stylistically and narratively, it is simply a rehash of what he did originally in *Artemio Cruz*, and not worth extensive analysis. Some critics feel, as a matter of fact, that most of Fuentes' famous "style" is very much an imitation (another "source") of Malcolm Lowry's *Under the Volcano*. From Faulkner to Lowry is not a long jump, but are we to allow Fuentes no originality at all?

27. *Excelsior*, Mexico, D. F., 2 March 1967, in the general news

columns; the dispatch is dated Barcelona, 1 March, and is credited to the Associated Press.

28. During my visit to Barcelona in the summer of 1967, Mr. Carlos Barral, of the publishing house mentioned, allowed me to examine the manuscript. It was 559 pages long, badly typed (apparently a first draft by Fuentes himself), and is dedicated to Aurora and Julio Cortázar, the Argentine novelist whose work and style Fuentes admires highly. I was given to understand by Mr. Barral that the reasons for the Spanish censor's disapproval, in addition to the so-called obscenity, were that it is "anti-German, anti-Catholic and pro-Jewish" (an example, if one is needed, of censorial "overkill").

29. Robert G. Mead, Jr., "Carlos Fuentes, airado novelista mexicano," *Hispania*, May 1967, pp. 229-35.

30. *Ibid.*, p. 234 (my translation).

31. *Ibid.*

32. George R. McMurray, *"Cambio de piel*, An Existentialist Novel of Protest," *Hispania*, March 1969, pp. 150-54.

33. John Fowles' *Collector* and *The Magus* come to mind in connection with this statement—*The Magus*, published in 1965, shows great similarities of themes to *A Change of Skin*.

34. McMurray, *op. cit.*, p. 152.

35. Since writing this (1969), Fuentes has returned to Mexico to live — whether "permanently" or not will depend on the mood of a very moody personality.

Chapter Nine

1. Glanville, Brian, "Speaking of Books: What Else Writers Should Do," *The New York Times Book Review*, Sunday, April 23, 1967, pp. 2 and 44-45. He quotes Connolly, p. 2.

2. Also quoted in Glanville's article, *supra*, p. 2.

3. *Ibid.*, p. 44.

4. *Playbill*, Vol. 1, No. 11, Nov. 1964, 5-12. This article was written directly in English by Fuentes. This quote: p. 6.

5. *Ibid.*, p. 7.

6. I am much indebted to the assistant librarian of the *Hemeroteca*, Mrs. Lidia de Guzmán, for her help in "browsing."

7. *Siempre!*, No. 631, July 28, 1965, Supplement p. VII.

8. Harss & Dohmann, *op. cit.*, pp. 281-82.

9. *Life en Español,* Aug. 1, 1966, pp. 54-61.

Chapter Ten

1. René Wellek, *Concepts of Criticism* (New Haven, 1963), see especially the last essay, pp. 344-64.

2. *Ibid.,* p. 18. Wellek distinguishes at least six general trends in literary criticism, all new in the last half-century: (1) Marxist, (2) pyschoanalytic, (3) linguistic and stylistic, (4) organistic formalism, (5) myth, resting on the results of cultural anthropology and the speculations of Carl Jung, and (6) philosophical, based on Existentialism and kindred world views (pp. 345-46).

3. Both quotations are from Bacon (Wallace, A.) & Breen (Robt. S.), *Literature as Experience* (New York, 1959), pp. 107-8.

4. C. S. Lewis, *An Experiment in Criticism* (Cambridge [England], 1961), p. 19.

5. *Ibid.,* p. 123.

6. The whole question of whether a creative artist is actually aware of the "steps" in the creative process has fascinated critics almost since the beginning of criticism, but is too complicated, apparently, to be solved on the basis of our present knowledge of the conscious and unconscious minds; in the case of Fuentes, of any modern "intellectual" writer, the process is probably not only conscious but largely deliberate, otherwise there would be no "experimental" writing as such. A tangential consideration with Fuentes is that the term "experimental" has become simply a name for a style: what may be discussed as "experimental" in *Artemio Cruz* is hardly so any longer in *A Change of Skin.*

7. In speaking of a bullfight Lea says, for example, that the fans "armed a scandal"—a direct translation of the Spanish idiom, *armar un escándalo*—obviously an attempt to convey ambience through style.

8. Quoted by Carballos in his *Diecinueve . . .* etc. (see Chapter 8, Note 7), p. 433.

9. *Ibid.,* p. 431-32.

Selected Bibliography

PRIMARY SOURCES

1. Works by Carlos Fuentes

The name, publisher, place, and date of the first Spanish edition will be given first. If there has been an English translation, the data for that publication will be given second (if there has been no translation, only a rendering of the title in English will be given).

The Short Stories:

1. *Los días enmascarados* (Mexico: Los Presentes, 1954). (Los Presentes was a publishing house, of short duration, founded by Juan José Arreola especially for young writers. There was also a Studium edition published the same year.) ("The Masked Days").
2. *Cantar de ciegos* (Mexico: Editorial Joaquín Mortiz, S. A., 1964). ("Song of the Blind").

The Novels

1. *La región más transparente* (Mexico: Fondo de Cultura Económica, 1958). *(Where the Air is Clear* [New York: Ivan Obolensky, Inc., 1960]).
2. *Las buenas consciencias* (Mexico: Fondo de Cultura Económica, 1959). *(The Good Conscience* [New York: Ivan Obolensky, Inc., 1961]).
3. *La muerte de Artemio Cruz* (Mexico: Fondo de Cultura Económica, 1962). *(The Death of Artemio Cruz* [New York: Farrar, Straus, 1964]).
4. *Aura* [Mexico: Era (Alacena), 1962]. *(Aura)*.
5. *Zona sagrada* (Mexico: Siglo XXI [Mexico Veintiuno] Editores, 1967). *(Sacred Zone* [or *Sanctuary* or *Home Base])*.
6. *Cambio de piel* (Mexico: Editorial Joaquín Mortiz, S. A., 1967). *(A Change of Skin* [New York: Farrar, Strauss & Giroux, 1967]).

The Other Writings

To try to make anything like a complete listing of Fuentes'
articles, political essays, topical reviews, script work, etc., would
be little short of impossible, since he has written and published
such work all over Europe and the Western Hemisphere, from
Russia to Chile, Argentina, Cuba, Central America, the United
States, and most, of course, in Mexico. The Spanish-speaking
reader is referred especially to the catalogue and collection in the
Hemeroteca Nacional in Mexico City, and to such publications
as those of the Universidad Autónoma de México, *Siempre!,*
Política (before 1962), *Life en Español, etc.* The English-speaking reader will find Fuentes' work in *Holiday, Show, The Nation,*
Monthly Review, and other current periodicals. He has written
and published scores, if not hundreds, of articles of varying
length on almost every conceivable subject.

SECONDARY SOURCES

The following selective listing includes biographical and critical
writings useful to a student of Fuentes' work, and indications as
to where to find additional material.

Bibliographically, the first five chapters of this study are
thoroughly covered in my work titled *México épico* (Mexico:
Costa-Amic, 1962), pp. 269-76, where the interested student can
find scores of useful titles that will facilitate further reading in
the material covered in the background chapters.

The following have also been useful in the preparation of
this study:

BOTSFORD, KEITH. "My Friend Fuentes," *Commentary,* Feb. 1965.
    An article on Fuentes' attitudes towards literature and his
    "failure" in *Artemio Cruz;* interesting for its pointed crit-
    icism of Fuentes in a personal vein.

CARBALLO, EMMANUEL. *Cuentistas mexicanos modernos* (Mexico:
    Libro-Mex Editores, S. de R. L., 1956). A series of critical
    essays on modern Mexican short story writers, by a man
    who was co-editor (with Fuentes) of the *Revista Mexicana*
    de Literatura.

————. *Diecinueve protagonistas de la literatura mexicana del siglo XX* (Mexico: Empresas editoriales, S. A., 1965). A collection of critical essays on nineteen representative writers of twentieth-century Mexican literature.

HARSS, LUIS & DOHMANN, BARBARA. "Carlos Fuentes or the New Heresey," *Into the Mainstream* (New York: Harper & Row, 1967). The most valuable essay on Fuentes to date—it evaluates his work and gives much valuable data about his life.

MCMURRAY, GEORGE R. "*Cambio de piel*, An Existential Novel of Protest," *Hispania*, March, 1969, pp. 150-54. An appraisal of Fuentes' latest novel from a critico-philosophical point of view.

MEAD, ROBERT J., JR. "Carlos Fuentes, Mexico's Angry Novelist," *Books Abroad*, XXXVIII, No. 4 (Autumn, 1964), 380-82. An estimate of Fuentes' work up to the year 1964.

————. "Literature and Politics: Our Image and Our Policy in Latin America," *Hispania*, May, 1966, pp. 302-7. An article on U. S. mistakes in Latin America; deals with Fuentes indirectly.

————. "Carlos Fuentes, airado novelista mexicano," *Hispania*, May, 1967, pp. 229-35. A reworking of the first Mead article listed above, in Spanish.

REEVE, RICHARD M. "Aura," *Hispania*, May, 1966, p. 355. A critical review of one of Fuentes' most important novels.

In addition to the above, Richard L. Jackson of Carleton University, in *Revista Iberoamericana*, Jul.-Dec., 1965, pp. 297-301, has collected a listing of articles by and about Fuentes, titled "Hacia una Bibliografía de y sobre Carlos Fuentes" (Toward a Bibliography of and about Carlos Fuentes). He lists Fuentes' major works as of that year, plus (in Section C) some seven titles of Prologues, Articles, Reviews, and Essays by Fuentes; and in Section II, he lists further some forty-four titles about Carlos Fuentes, mostly reviews of one or another of Fuentes' novels or articles that refer to him in passing in connection with some consideration of Latin-American literature. These articles are of value or interest chiefly to the academician who may wish to make a comparison of opinions on Fuentes.

Since the above was prepared and written, Richard M. Reeve, a scholar previously mentioned and quoted, has published "An Annotated Bibliography on Carlos Fuentes: 1949-69" in *Hispania*, October, 1970 (Vol. 53), pp. 597-652. This would seem to be a definitive listing of Carlos Fuentes' literary production for the years given.

Index